The 7 Assumptions That Drive Success & Happiness

The 7 Assumptions That Drive Success & Happiness

Jimmy Brown, PhD

The 7 Assumptions That Drive Success & Happiness

ISBN-13: 978-0-692-07159-5 (sc)
ISBN-10: 0-692-07159-8

Printed in the United States of America

Contents

Figures

Acknowledgments

I would like to quickly acknowledge all the wonderful people that I have had the opportunity to work with over the past 20+ years, some of whom may even recognize themselves in these stories. Your knowledge, wisdom, and friendships mean the world.

I would also like to acknowledge the Central Arkansas Human Resources Association, the West Little Rock Rotary, and the Accounting & Finance Woman's Alliance. These organizations graciously permitted me to share these concepts while still in development, and their participants' feedback was extremely beneficial in finalizing the results.

Introduction

Many of us were taught as children to never, ever assume. We were told that assuming was rude. We were told that assuming was dangerous. My personal favorite was the warning that when you assume, you make an *ASS* out of *U* and *ME*. In short, we were led to believe that making assumptions is a very bad thing indeed.

But what actually happens when we assume? Why are assumptions something we must avoid? Why do we need to be so careful to never, ever make them? Why are we taught so early on that they are very bad things?

According to *Webster's Dictionary*, the noun form of "assumption" is either the act of assuming, such as when an idea or statement is accepted as true without proof (1996). The verb form of "assume" relates to doing one of three things:

- To take upon oneself, as in to assume responsibility for some action or outcome

- To affect, as in to assume an attitude

- To take for granted without any proof

I suspect that the aspect of assuming that our parents and teachers cautioned us against was primarily focused on the act of taking something for granted without any support for it necessarily being true. In particular, they were recommending we avoid assumptions that could potentially lead to undesirable outcomes. An example would be when a teenager assumes it's okay to throw a party while his parents are out of town just because the parents never explicitly forbade it. So, the teenager invites a few friends, who assume it is okay to invite a few of *their* friends, who in turn assume it is okay to invite a few more friends. And pretty soon, that teenager finds himself in an out-of-control situation that looks like something out of a bad B movie. While the responsibility for this outcome clearly rests with the teenager who made the wrong assumption, the case could also be made that the teenager's parents share some guilt due to their assumption that their child should know better than to do such a thing. That, however, is probably not a line of reasoning that would do the teenager too much good once his parents got home.

Unlike the preceding example, where an assumption can cause someone to not think through their possible outcomes and thereby lose control of their life, there are assumption that can be beneficial—for example, when the word assumption is related to taking responsibilities upon ourselves, affecting the various aspects of our lives. When used this way, the word actually becomes very useful and powerful. If we try to identify assumptions that may help focus our lives, we realize that there are certain truths about ourselves and the world around us which, if we accept them, can lead to happier and more successful lives. The question is: What are those assumptions, how do we apply them, and how to we manage them? This book attempts to answer those questions.

Before we get into that, however, we must attend to one of the rules of good scholarship and provide the context from which this book is written. It is written from the perspective of someone who worked his way through college, and then went on to obtain advanced degrees in Psychology and Organizational Development. For nearly two decades, I primarily worked as a management consultant with a focus on human capital, organizational change, and business strategy.

During my consulting career, I interacted with everyone from CEOs to janitors and dealt with just about every kind of person you can think of. I also kept regular notes and journals in one form or another. While some were in more depth than others, many of the day-to-day entries captured not only what I did, but also my observations and insights about the people I worked with as well. In particular, if I noticed someone who seemed to be doing particularly well, I took note of it. At the time, I always thought I would come back later and see what I could learn from them, but most of the time I forgot about it and moved on to the next consulting engagement.

Because of changing family obligations, my work life evolved from being a road warrior management consultant who taught a few college courses on the side to spending more and more of my time in higher education. As I got further into my academic career, I found myself doing more teaching and supervising more research in areas like leadership, happiness, and success. The more I got into these topics, the more I started thinking about the various people I had worked with over the years. While I won't be so bold as to claim that everyone I worked with was happy and successful, I had the honor and privilege to work with what seemed to be an atypical number of individuals who fit into one or both of those categories. Reflecting on those experiences is where this journey began.

My first step was to comb through the various notes and journals I collected over the years. I paid special attention to commonalities among the various individuals I had worked with so that I could identify themes that provide insight into what drives success and happiness. As I did, I realized that one key differentiator between those who led happy and successful lives and those who did not is that the successful people seemed to operate from a certain set of core assumptions. These assumptions drove their daily interactions, as well as their reactions when challenges presented themselves. It is these assumptions that gave them the framework to be successful and happy.

This is not to say that any of these people ever told me that they woke up each day saying, "I am going to assume X." In fact, there was no one place in my notes where a single person ever claimed that there was some magical set of assumptions that guided their approach to life. What they did instead was to share stories about things they had learned throughout the course of their lives and professional careers. As I reviewed my notes from many of these conversations, I realized that the lessons learned could be coalesced into seven basic assumptions:

1st Assumption: Success is a self-defined social construction.

2nd Assumption: Your story is a first-person narrative.

3rd Assumption: Life is always in progress.

4th Assumption: You are going to have ups and downs.

5th Assumption: No person is an island.

6th Assumption: It seemed like a good idea at the time.

7th Assumption: You will become who you surround yourself with.

****

While these *7 Assumptions* did not come from a single formalized research project, they did evolve through a combination of two processes that professional researchers call *grounded theory* and *phenomenological research* (Creswell, 2013). In more down-to-earth terms, when I reviewed the various journal entries and notes I had amassed over the years, I looked for ideas that hung together. I looked for things that were mutually exclusive and collectively exhaustive. To illustrate the volume of material I looked through, the picture shown in Figure 1 is just a small sampling of the personal journals and notes I reviewed.

Figure 1. Photo of Some Notes.

After I reviewed these notes and got a firm grasp on the themes presented, I then looked for proven theoretical constructs that could help me understand and explain those trends. I started this process by looking through books on subjects like social psychology, orgranizational beheavior, and executive coaching. I then looked at peer-reviewed academic journals such as the *Journal of Applied Psychology*, the *Journal of Applied Behavioral Science*, *Administrative Science Quarterly*, and *The OD Practitioner*. While I was doing all this, I also conducted several formal interviews with executive and leaders I had access to so that I could flesh out and clarify some of my early ideas. After all that, I combined those trends into a framework that can be used and applied by anyone with the drive to do so. The result of those efforts are the *7 Assumptions* in this book. Each of the assumptions is addressed in a separate chapter.

****

As a quick side note before we go any further, I feel I should make a point about there being "seven" assumptions. As we look through the different books and concepts in this domain, there seems to be a notable proponderance of the number seven. There the *Seven Habits of Highley Effective People,* of course. Deepka Chopra published *The Seven Spiritual Laws of Success.* Sean Anchor's *The Happiness Advantage* focuses on seven principles of positive psychology. There is also the McKinsey 7S model of strategic planning, and numerous other related paradigms that seem to relate to the number seven. The number seven seems to be everywhere. Discounting the idea that it is some magical and spiritual number that holds power over our lives, I actually made a concerted effort to try to structure this book into five, six, eight, or even nine assumptions just to avoid it coming out with seven. I really didn't want to work with seven because I didn't want it to look like I was just copying everyone else. Being a behavioral scientist first and foremost, however, I am a firm believer that we should follow the data wherever it leads, regardless of whether that is where we want to go or not. Attending to that principle, we did end up with these *7 Assumptions*. And to be honest, the more I've reread this thing (as is normal in the writing process), the more these seven ideas make sense.

****

Whenever I read a *self-help* book—and I've read many—I often wonder if the authors actually practice what they preach. Did Stephen Covey truly follow his seven habits? Does Tony Robbins really awaken his inner giant? Does Richard Carlson actually not sweat the small stuff? I'm skeptical by nature, and my training as a behavioral scientiest only increases that cynicism. And I'm sure at least a few people reading this text will ask the same thing about me. Does Dr. Jimmy Brown, PhD really follow these *7 Assumptions* on a daily basis? For those people, I feel compelled to answer honestly: "not always, but I am trying." But then again, that is kind of the point.

As human beings, we are infinately fallable, but also have unlimited potential. In an effort to find ways to fullfill my own potential, I began this journey by asking critical questions of myself. When I examined the answers to those questions, I realized that I could begin operating from a set of assumptions that would allow me to interact with myself and the world more effectively. I would also have to recognize, as we'll discuss with our *4th Assumption*, that I'll be more successful on some days than on others. That is okay, however, becauase as we will learn with our *3rd Assumption*, life is always a work in progess, and the most important thing you can do is *begin*. Most importantly, no matter how far off-track you may feel about reaching your goal, the sooner you course-correct, the sooner you'll get back on track. And always being ready to get back on track is one of the key elements of being successful and happy.

1st Assumption: Success Is a Self-Defined Social Construction

Everyone says they want to be successful, but what *is* success? Is it financial security? Is it a loving and caring spouse or life partner? Is it the respect of peers and colleagues? The details depend on who is asking, and who is answering, that question. The answer may even change from time to time.

Webster's (1996) defines success in three ways:

- The achievement of something desired, intended, or attempted

- The gaining of fame and prosperity

- One that succeeds

I find these definitions lack utility because one does not necessarily have to have fame to be successful, and defining success as "one that succeeds" sounds like circular logic. More importantly, *Webster's* does not hold a monopoly on defining success. Tony Robbins defines success as "living your life in a way that causes you to feel tons of pleasure and very little pain"

(1991). This definition seems like something of a hedonistic approach to me, but it is a standard many people aspire to. Of course, I'm sure we can all think of people who have pursued this ideal of success and not met with favorable results.

If we look at success from a psychological perspective, we could describe it as meeting some standard that one holds or that implies others' favorable evaluations of oneself (Wood et al., 2005). This definition of success is also problematic because we have to deal with the question of who sets these standards and what happens if the circumstances that these standards are applied to change. Moreover, part of this definition implies that we take other people's opinions into account when we define success. As we'll talk about in a little bit, using other people's terms to define your own success can be risky.

One of the most amusing definitions of success comes from Friedrich Nietzsche, who was once quoted as saying that "success is always being a big liar" (Esar, 1968). I doubt that he was saying that one's success is defined by just being a liar, but what he was more likely claiming was that to achieve success, we have to be dishonest and deceitful. Nietzsche seemed to believe that we could only succeed by taking advantage of others and winning at any cost. While this definition of success does make a modicum of sense when placed in the context of

Nietzsche's other work, this kind of zero sum game approach does not work for success in our modern world, in no small part due to our *5th Assumption:* No person is an island. While the Nietzschean approach may result in a few quick wins in a small number of cases, trying to apply this longer term will always result in less than desirable outcomes. Our goal here is to understand success so that we can maximize the desirable outcomes in the long run.

Clearly, there are a lot of different definitions of success. The reason for having so many different definitions is that success is not something we can objectively measure, like temperature or distance. Success is a subjective construct that is based upon interpersonal agreement and implicit understanding, usually derived from some shared history and common experience. In other words, we construct our definitions of success because we have at some point agreed that doing or achieving *X, Y, and Z* means that we are successful. This is what postmodern psychologists call a social construction (Hatch & Cuntliff, 2013).

While there have always been social constructions, the idea that we can create and manipulate our own definitions of reality became popular with psychologists and other behavioral scientists in the late 1960s; the concept was based upon the work of people like Peter Berger, Thomas Luckmann, and Karl Weick (Gergen, 2001; Hatch & Cuntliff, 2013). It was a reaction to the *modernist* or *objectivist* view of the world, which focused on logic, reason, and objectivity. The basic premise is that the objectivist view is far too limiting, and that the world is actually made up of subjective perceptions, not necessarily concrete truths. The school of thought also encompasses the belief that accepting the ideal of a concrete and objective reality has somehow led to many of the world's ills and social injustices. Despite the way that the political climate has evolved over the last few years, however, that is not a debate we are going to tackle here. What we *will* tackle is how we can use these concepts to drive happiness and success.

Despite its popularity among academics and philosophers, many people find the concept of social constructionism to be somewhat heady. It is the kind of cogitation that is usually only embraced by college professors and hipsters who spend way too much time in trendy coffee shops. Its ins and outs give people headaches, and someone who is a concrete thinking either finds it ridiculous or impossible to understand.

It becomes much easier to understand, however, when we think about it in terms of what I like to call the table example. In this example, someone who takes an objective view of the world would say that a table is a table is a table. You can put food on it and eat off it, you can put things on it until you need them later, and you can even do work at it—but it is always a table. A social constructionist, however, says that a table is only a table because we have all *agreed* that it is a table. If we agree to lie down and go to sleep on it, it becomes a bed. If we agree to stand up and dance on it, it becomes a stage. If we agree to sit under it in the rain, it becomes shelter.

While this is an interesting idea, this approach quickly becomes problematic if taken too far and applied in the wrong context. For example, if we sleep on a table too often, we may wake up with an aching back. If we try to dance on a table, we may fall off and get hurt. If we try to use a table as shelter from the rain, we are going to get much wetter than if we had just gone inside. Obviously, there are some real problems applying this concept to objects that we can touch, feel, or taste. But when dealing with things we cannot touch or taste, like success, the idea actually becomes very useful and somewhat liberating.

Far too often, people accept that success is an object that can only be defined one way. They usually base those definitions on some imagined standards, or worse yet, other people's expectations. Driven by these expectations, they pursue outcomes that don't lead to success, but instead result in frustration, misery, and failure. I'm sure we've all known people who have let their parents', spouse's, or someone else's definition of success cause them to make choices they would not have made otherwise. They chase outcomes that don't really matter to them because someone else says they should. As a result; they can't get excited, can't commit, and are unable to achieve their goals. If you can't stay excited and committed to something, the likelihood of success goes down significantly, and eventual failure becomes almost inevitable. All because they let someone else socially construct their definition of success rather than constructing it themselves.

****

Now that we have established that there are a lot of different ways to define success, and that it is a bad idea to let someone else define it for us, we must start asking what success really means to us. This is actually a very difficult question, because if we agree that our definition is something that we socially construct, and we need to do it ourselves, then does this not mean that anyone who says they are successful is correct regardless of the state of their life? The honest answer is "sort of, but not really."

While success is difficult to define due to all the different ways to qualify as successful, most people would agree that it is pretty easy to spot someone who is *un*successful. They usually meet at least one of three standards:

- They are unhappy

- They can't pay their bills to take care of themselves (or their family)

- They are a burden on those around them, be that family, friends, or society in general

Using these three standards, it is possible to deduce what a successful person is by defining what a successful person is not and then flip-flopping it. This is a logical reasoning process that scientists refer to as *falsification* (Chalmers, 2013). It allows us to come to a conclusion about something by determining what facts about it are false. Using this approach, we can reason that someone who meets the opposite of those three criteria is successful. Given that, we can now say that for someone to be classified as successful, they must pass three tests:

- Overall, they are happy with their lives

- They can support themselves financially, as well as their family if they have one

- They are not a burden on other people

One would think that passing the first of these three tests would not be hard. In reality, however, we all know people who are generally unhappy in their jobs, their relationships, or just their lives in general. Maybe they made some bad decisions. Maybe they've had some bad breaks. Maybe they just don't know what they want out of life and, as such, are unable to make the decisions that they need to in order to become happy. Regardless of the reason, they simply feel they aren't getting to where they want to be.

When I give talks on these concepts, I often get asked about people who can pass the second or third test but not the first. Do we consider those people to be successful? The answer to that question is "no" for two very important reasons. First, to be successful, you must be benefiting yourself. If you are not happy, you are not benefiting yourself. The second reason is because if you are not happy, it will only be a matter of time before you will find yourself unable to meet the second and third criteria.

How many times have we seen people who have great jobs, make lots of money, have all the right toys—and yet seem totally miserable? More importantly, how often have we watched those same people self-destruct, usually because something important was missing, to the point where they were willing to risk all they had achieved? Even though they look like they are leading a great life from the outside, to them, there is still something missing. That hole has to be filled with something. If they can't fill it with something positive, they almost always find something negative. It may be drugs, it may be alcohol, it may be extramarital affairs, or any other non-positive thing. It happens far too often. If you have been lucky enough to not personally know someone who has done this, just go pick up any celebrity magazine or check out TMZ.com. You will find plenty of examples.

If the first, and most important, part of being successful is being happy, what does it take to achieve that? The answer depends on each individual's social construction. While there are well-established broad categories of factors that contribute to happiness, the truth is that what makes one person happy may be very different from what makes another person happy. One person may be driven by a high need for achievement. Another person may be driven by wanting to contribute something to the global good. Still another person may simply want to raise a well-adjusted family and coach their kid's soccer team. When you get right down to it, happiness is about a set of individual preferences related to how people meet certain basic needs.

****

One of the first people to study those needs was humanistic psychologist Abraham Maslow, who classified peoples' needs into five basic categories (Schultz & Schultz, 2016). These categories start with the most basic physiological needs like food and water, and gradually increase in complexity and subjectivity to what Maslow terms "self-actualization." This is Maslow's fancy way of saying that we are being all we can be and fullfilling our fullest potential in all areas. We are not going to worry about self-actuallization here because it is a debatable topic at best, and Malsow himself said only around 1% of people ever achieve this. It is relevant to our discussion, however, because it helps frame the complete hierarchy, illustrated in Figure 2.

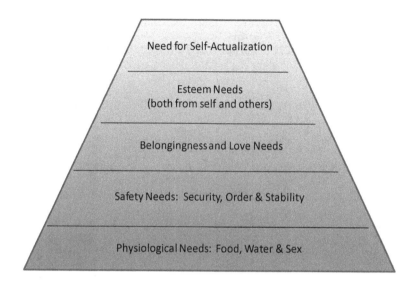

Figure 2. Maslow's Hierarchy of Needs. Adapted from Schultz & Schultz (2016).

Maslow's hierarchy has been somewhat controversial over the years, largely due to his supposition that before a person can address the needs of any particular level, they must first completely fulfill the needs at the preceeding levels. For example, Maslow posits that before someone can worry about their *Belongingness* needs, they must first take care of all their *Physiological* and *Safety* needs. Before someone can take care of their *Esteem* needs, they must first fully address thier *Belongingness* needs. Moreover, Maslow suggested that if some lower-level needs were previously met but the situation changes to where they no longer are, the person must start all over again. While this kind of linear thinking is useful when trying to explain this concept to freshman psychology students or create a diagram, it can become fairly problematic when we try to fit it into real-world applications such as self-improvement.

People's needs and wants are not as simple as some assembly process where you can do step 1, then step 2, then step 3. Dealing with people's needs and wants is much more complicated due to what Peter Senge refers to as *detail* and *dynamic complexities* (2006). *Detail complexity* means that there are many variables to deal with. *Dynamic complexity* means that the causes and effects may be subtle and the interaction between the two may not be immediately obvious. In simple terms, these complexities mean that each person has a lot of unique experiences and history, and because of this, each person's needs are distinctive. In addition, as we'll discuss in our *3rd Assumption*, meeting those needs is usually not a one-shot deal but an ongoing cycle. Often, you may meet needs at one level of Malsow's hierachy and then have to revisit the needs at a prevoius level at some later time due to changing dynamics and/or details. If we were to strictly follow Malsow's hierachy, this would a problem because we would have to constantly start over. To avoid this problem, we are going to tweak and modify his thought process to make it more managable for our purposes.

****

The bottom two rungs of the ladder, *Physiological* and *Safety* needs, are really about what is necessary to maintain health, safety, and sanity. Another way to think about these needs is to ask what is required for you to avoid being stressed out about yourself and your family's wellbeing. This gets into things like having a stable job, a house in a safe neighborhood, food on the table, and enough savings that you're not living paycheck to paycheck. Obviously, there are lots of different inputs that affect these needs (i.e., *detail complexity*), so these needs can vary greatly from person to person. In addition, these needs are *dynamic* enough to also vary from time to time in a given person's life. For example, a $35,000 a year salary and a one-bedroom apartment may meet all of the *Physiological* and *Safety* needs of a single person in their early 20s who is living in a small town. That exact same income level and living conditions would likely come nowhere near meeting the needs of someone in their late 30s with a spouse and three small childern in a major city.

The paradox is that while failing to meet these needs can be stressful and unhealthy, having a hyperfocus on exceeding these needs can also be stressful and unhealthy. For example, we need food and water to live, but the obseity problem in the United States proves that consuming too much will not make you happier or healthier. A lack of safety and security will make one stressed, but anyone burdened with obsessive compulsive disorder (OCD) can attest to the fact that allowing yourself to become overfixated can cause a whole host of other problems. The key is to make sure we meet these needs at a level that *sustains* us, but not at a level that *contains* us. For this reason, we will classify all the needs in this group as our *Sustainment* needs.

To recap, while we know that not meeting our *Sustainment* needs will make us unhappy, feeling too much presure to exceed them also creates issues. The key is maintaining equilibrium between too little and too much. To understand how to achieve that balance, we have to apply what we will term the *stress threshold*. While we will talk more about stress when we get to our *2nd Assumption*, the point here is that even though not meeting your minimum *Sustainment* needs will prevent you from being happy, setting your goals for those needs so high that it causes you be stressed will also prevent you from being happy. The stress comes from both continually feeling unsatisfied due to never meeting those important needs and wants, and from the amount of extra effort required to keep trying. This is in addition to losing focus on meeting other needs. Figure 3 illustrates this concept.

Figure 3. Sustainment Needs and Stress Thresholds

Now that we have extablished the bottom two rungs of Maslow's hierarchy as *Sustainment* needs, we must next define how we will manage the other levels so that those also *sustain* us but not *contain* us. To understand this, we must remember that *Sustainment* needs are about *what* we need to avoid being unhappy. These are the tangible, objective things that will allow us to feel safe and secure and to function in a healthy way. The other levels in Maslow's hierarchy are about the *hows* of going about meeting our needs to be happy.

Our *how* needs are based upon what each person values, and what each person's values are. For example, if you value lots of communication and direct interaction with other people, trying to meet your needs through a job that keeps you alone in a cube all day probably won't be a very good fit for you. In addition, if someone has very high moral values, being in a position where they are having to deal with people and situations they consider to be immoral could also be a problem. One of the more interesting examples of this was several years ago when the consulting firm I worked for received a request for proposal (RFP) from a media company that produced what we'll call adult male-oriented content. The vice president of the media team was fairly religious and had no interest in working for a client that he found morally objectionable. While there was a little debate about if we should just let someone else lead the effort, the decision was to made to decline to respond in support of the VP. In the end, we all agreed that *how* we worked together as a team was as important as *what* we achieved.

While these *how* needs do vary from person to person, the key point is that they are based upon each person's individual values and how they would prefer to go about their day. For simplicity's sake, we are going to group these needs into what we will call our *Values* needs. We will do an exercise in the next chapter that will help us gain a better understanding of those needs, but for now just recognize that Figure 4 illustrates how we have modified Malsow's hierarcy for our discussion. Going forward, we will only refernce our *Sustainment* and *Values* needs.

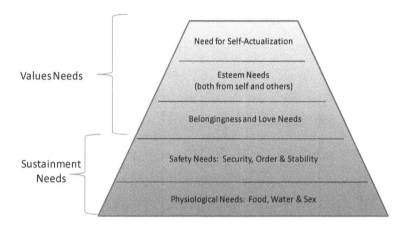

Figure 4. Modified Maslow's Hierarchy of Needs

The important takeaway here is that the *Sustainment* needs are our most basic needs and form the *what* of being happy. They are typically more tangible and can be assessed objectively. Failing to meet those will cause us to be unhappy, but meeting or even exceeding those needs will not necessarily make us happier. This is often due to the extra effort and stress required to keep exceeding those needs over a long period of time.

Our *Values* needs are the *how* of being happy. They are typically intangible and more subjective. Meeting those needs will only make us happy if we express them in a way that allows us to meet our *Sustainment* needs. For example, if you value the opportunity to expresss yourself and be appreciated for that artistic expression (i.e., Maslow's esteem needs) but you are working as accountant and don't ever have any kind of outlet to do that, you can meet and exceed your *Sustainment* needs all day long, but you will never be happy because you are not addressing what you value. On the other hand, if you have the same needs but decide to be a starving artist all your life, you'll probably also never be happy because you'll be stressed out wondering where your next meal is coming from. In other words, you will be unable to sustain yourself (unless, of course, you are lucky enough to have a big trust fund or something).

In these kinds of situations, it is important to find some way to meet the *Values* needs to some degree while also being able to meet the *Sustainment* needs. Some people do this through finding outlets outside of the activities they do to meet their *Sustainment* needs. These are the people who paint or play in bar bands after they finish their "day jobs." Another approach is to find some way to meet your *Sustainment* needs by leveraging the passions that are your *Values* needs. This is how people choose careers like graphic artists and high school drama teachers.

Why is it so important to understand both our *Sustainment* needs and our *Values* needs? Because it is only through that understanding that we can find ways to be happy that allow us to also pay our bills, and thereby not be burdens on society and those around us. As we have already established, once we pass those three tests, we can be considered successful, and being successful is how we all want to tell our story.

Jimmy Brown, PhD

2nd Assumption: Your Life Is a First-Person Narrative

As we all learned in English class, there are three ways to tell a story—first, second, and third person narratives. The first-person narrative is where the main actor describes the events from his or her own perspective. Second-person narrative where the author talks directly to the reader. They are not that common in literature, but what we're doing right now is a perfect example. Third-person narrative is when someone besides the author tells the story. There are two types of this approach. There is third person limited where someone who is part of the story, but not the main character, tells the story. My personal favorite example of this approach is *The Great Gatsby*. Then there is a third-person omniscient narrative where some kind of all-knowing, unseen entity tells the story as we watch it unfold. A critical point that these definitions sometimes omit is that that *storyteller is the one who controls the pace, the flow, and the outcomes of the story*. As such, *who* tells the story is very important.

Ideally, your life should be a first-person narrative. This means that *you* are the main actor and *you* should decide how the story will be told. This is the way it is meant to be, and this is the way it *should* be because, as we've already learned, you are the only one who truly understands your *Values Needs* and your *Sustainment Needs*. As such, you are the only one who can decide if you are happy and successful.

There are, however, times when life is not a first-person narrative because someone else decides what is going to happen to you, thereby creating a third-person limited narrative where someone else controls your story. This is okay when we are children and our parents are telling our story because we are still learning about life, but as we grow to adulthood, this quickly becomes unhealthy.

There are also times when life just unfolds around us, thereby creating a third-person omniscient narrative where some unseen hand controls your story. While there are certain theological perspectives that appear to promote the value of surrendering our lives over to second- and third-person narrative (e.g., Calvinism), the truth is that deeper examination usually reveals that these philosophies recommend embracing a higher calling and moralistic standard, not giving up and just letting things just happen. As such, for the remainder of this discussion, we will presume that we all agree that our lives should be a first-person narrative and will only focus on how to manage things according to that assumption.

One of the first things many counseling psychologists tell their clients is that you can't control other people, only how you react to them. What this means is that regardless of our needs, our wants, or our actions, we can't make other people do anything they are not willing to do. We have no more and no less power over them than they implicitly or explicitly choose to grant us. We may try to influence them through punishment or reward, but we cannot exert dominating authority without their agreement to care about those punishments or rewards.

By the same token, no one in this world actually controls you but *you*. Yes, you too can be influenced, or even coerced, by people like parents, teachers, bosses, and government officials. This influence often comes in the form of anticipating positive benefits for compliance, and fearing negative consequences for noncompliance. If you don't care about the benefits or consequences of doing what someone asks, however, then those other people really don't have any power over you at all. One of the best examples of this paradigm is young children who have no fear of their parents and behave like holy terrors. Because they have no fear, they disregard any requests by their parents for compliance. If we want to be free of the influence of others, we have to simply decide to be like those kids and no longer care about any rewards or punishments related to our behaviors.

This is not to say that you should go around engaging in whatever shenanigans you want. Everyone doing that would result in chaos, and every action we take does have some consequence or another. What it does mean, however, is that we are each the masters of our own destiny. If we go back to our narrative metaphor, each one of us tells our story from the perspectives of I's, me's and we's. By virtue of our choices and actions, we can choose endings that are happy or sad, joyous or painful, exciting or boring. We can even choose to make dramatic changes from one chapter to the next. It all depends on what we want our story to be and the kind of characters we want to play.

****

You will note that I used the plural form of the word "characters" rather than the singular. I used this plural form because we all play multiple roles at different times in our lives and in different situations. For example, the role I play around my wife and children as *husband and father* is very different than the role I play around my friends as *one of the guys*. Both of these are different from the role I play at work as a *trusted advisor* to clients and colleagues. All three of those roles are different from the ones I play with my students as a *professor and mentor*. How I act, talk, and even dress varies from situation to situation depending on what I understand my role in that narrative to be, and the actions I need to take to be effective in that situation.

One of the best examinations of this concept is sociologist Erving Goffman's seminal work, *The Presentation of Self in Everyday Life* (1959). Dr. Goffman extends the Shakespearian metaphor of *all the world is a stage* to describe how people present different faces as they interact with the world around them. Those faces are often driven by what they think other people expect of them, or what perceptions by others they think will be most beneficial. One of my favorite examples is people who keep *The New York Times* or *Bloomberg BusinessWeek* on a coffee table so their visiting friends will think they are hip and informed, but actually spend more time reading cheap romance novels or muscle car magazines that are hidden in the bedroom dresser.

We all have such guilty pleasures that we keep hidden. Many of us also have opinions and practices that we only share with ourselves and selected others. That is perfectly fine, and a key part of being successful and happy is learning to integrate those different selves into our whole being. Doing this is largely a question of accepting that we have different *selves* for different situations.

When thinking of different *selves*, the question often arises about which is our *true self?* Is it the hip person who can quote last month's essay in *The Economist* about the downfall of the original tech bubble and the ongoing risks associated with Web 2.0? Or is it the person who watches *Beavis and Butthead* reruns at 2 a.m. and laughs hysterically at their "insights"? While there are a few sociologists and psychologists who say you have to pick one or the other, or some amalgamation of the two, I am of the camp that says they are *both* the true self. And for that matter, who cares? As previously stated, your life is a self-defined social construction, and you are the one who tells your story. If you need several divergent characters to tell your story, then that's fine. Many people find that playing multiple roles over time makes for a richer and more powerful life experience.

There are, however, some who believe they have only one true self and refuse to be anything but what they see as that *true self*. Usually the *self* they choose to stick with is whichever one they think other people will perceive as the coolest or trendiest. Ironically, that *self* is usually the most annoying to other people. More often than not, it is also their least effective self. Even so, these individuals stick to their opinions and practices no matter what the situation and regardless of the consequences, and those consequences are often not entirely positive.

Goffman proposes that people who take this approach do so because they believe that if they allow themselves to be anything but this *ideal self,* they will succumb to the role(s) they are playing and no longer be able to return once they leave the situation that requires them to take on a modified role (1959). One of the newer terms that has developed to describe the reasons these individuals give for this approach is that they are just *keeping it real*. While there are times when *keeping it real* may be a moral or ethical imperative, for the most part it is just a matter of being scared and stubborn. And as we have all learned from Dave Chappelle, there are often times when keeping it real goes wrong.

For those who don't recall, *Chappelle's Show* did a series of skits that showed individuals who found themselves in situations where they were on the horns of a dilemma, having to either *play a role* or *keep it real*. In each of these cases, the situation had no moral or ethical implications and choosing to *keep it real* actually required more effort than playing along. Moreover, in every case, the person's choice to *keep it real* led to very, very unpleasant consequences. The question, of course, is why someone would make such bad decisions even though the likely consequences were easy to predict. In the case of *Chappelle's Show,* it's because it is funny. If you haven't seen these skits, I recommend looking them up on YouTube. If nothing else, it will be good for a laugh. In real life, however, the answer is a little more complicated.

Going back to Goffman's explanation, these bad decisions are often driven by fear of losing touch with what individuals consider to be their *ideal self.* While there are varying opinions about whether fear is a good or bad thing, it is a fact that fear is a very powerful motivator. Fear of negative consequences prevents us from doing lots of things we otherwise might. One of the most unpleasant things that can happen to someone is for them to lose their sense of self and their identity. Obviously, this fear is not entirely unreasonable, but there are ways to prevent it. The best way to combat this is to be confident in whatever your *true self* is (or selves are) so that you can effectively play whatever roles you need to get through your day-to-day life. To really understand how to do this, we must first recognize two facts.

The first fact is that we are each the sum of all our experiences. We are also the sum of the people we spend the most time with, but we will discuss that in our *7th Assumption*. For now, we must simply realize that how we grew up, what we've done over the course of our lives, and what we have seen and heard affects who we are and how we function. Much like other people, however, we can't control our past because it has already happened. We can only control how we react to it and what we learn from it. The ability to recognize and apply this insight is one of the reasons there are some people who experienced childhoods filled with every challenge imaginable, yet grow up to be amazingly successful, while there are others who have great childhoods yet grow up to be complete losers.

The other fact, which is closely related to the first, is that you will become your parents unless you make a conscious decision not to. This is not a new insight. As far back as 1734, Alexander Pope was quoted as saying, "As the twig is bent, so grows the tree...". To be clear, by "parents," I don't just mean your biological father and mother. While there are certain innate predispositions that may be genetically inherited, it is the influences of our father and mother figures and the habits and behaviors we learn from them in our formative years that influence how we grow and become adults. These figures can include aunts, uncles, teachers, coaches, neighbors, and whoever else takes us under their wing and takes a long-term vested interest in our development. The key takeaway is that you will become an amalgamation of these people whether you like it or not.

The trick is becoming a positive amalgamation, not a negative one. Another way of thinking about this would be to say that we want to retain all the good traits of our parental figures and discard all the bad ones. Sounds simple enough, but this is in fact quite challenging. The good news, however, is that the first step is simply realizing this and recognizing that focusing on retaining the good traits is critical, because failing to do so practically guarantees that the bad traits will become dominant. This is closely related to developing good and bad habits, as we'll discuss in our *3rd Assumption.*

The second step in becoming the best of our parents is developing a well-formed sense of self. Sense of self is really about recognizing and understanding all the things we have talked about so far. What are our *Sustainment Needs*, what are our *Values Needs*, what *roles* do we play throughout our daily lives, and what were the influences that made us who we are today? Once we have a sense of this information, we can begin to answer some very critical questions:

- What are our strengths?

- What are our blind spots (a positive way of saying weaknesses)?

- What are the areas where we can or need to improve?

- What causes us stress?

- What are our stress behaviors?

Strengths, *Blind Spots*, and *Areas for Improvement* are all different sides to the same coin. They are the knowledge, skills, and abilities (KSAs) that we apply toward meeting our needs and achieving our goals. When I do individual coaching, I spend a great deal of time working with individuals to gather data about these KSAs.

First, the coachee defines what they believe to be their *Strengths*, *Blind Spots*, and *Areas for Improvement*. We then use a 360-degree assessment to gather feedback from people who know the coachee so that we can understand how others see them. We also use particular psychological assessments to gather unbiased ratings on relevant KSAs. We do all this to develop a baseline of the person's capabilities so that we can then develop improvement plans and track progress over time.

While the data collection process in formal coaching arrangements is a fairly robust, detailed, and sometimes costly endeavor, you can begin developing your own simplified baseline through some honest self-examination. Just find a quiet spot and take out three sheets of paper. At the top of each sheet, write down one of the following three questions:

- What do I do well enough that other people admire and/or compliment me on how well I do it? (i.e., what are my strengths?)

- What am I not good at? (i.e., what are my blind spots?)

- What blind spots limit me from being able to achieve what I need to in order to be happy and successful? (i.e., what are my areas for improvement?)

On each piece of paper, list items that answer the question at the top of the page. Most people tend to have at least five to seven items on each page. Some people will stop at five. Some people will completely fill up each sheet. The exact number doesn't matter—it is the thinking about it that counts. It is also best to first look at your *Strengths*, then do *Blind Spots*, then do *Areas for Improvement*. The reason for this order is that there is a significant difference between *Blind Spots* and *Areas for Improvement*. While a *Blind Spot,* by definition, is anything you don't do well, some of them may not be things you need to worry about because they don't impact your ability to pass any of the three tests for being successful that we discussed under our *1st Assumption*. You should recognize them, and manage them so they don't negatively impact you, but you don't necessarily need to work on them right now.

Blind Spots that inhibit your ability to pass any one of the three tests for success, however, are *Areas for Improvement*. This means they are the KSAs that you need to improve in order to be happy, make enough money, or be better to those people around you. We will discuss the process for improvement when we get to the *3rd Assumption* in the next chapter. For now, however, we simply need to be able to identify those areas that need to be improved, because not doing so can create stressful situations, and operating under stress is never our most effective behavior. Figure 5 provides a very simplified example of what a *Strengths* list might look like.

What do I do well enough that other people admire and/or compliment me on how well I do it?
1) Stay calm under pressure
2) Help bring people together
3) Work really well on Excel
4) Make good presentations
5) Cook great cakes

Figure 5. Example of Strengths List

****

Once we have these lists, we'll need to figure out what to do with them. Before we can do that, however, we need to talk a bit about stress. Stress is a state that occurs when people are faced with demands from the environment that require them to change in some way (Darley et. al., 1986). From a physiological standpoint, stress causes increased heart rate and respiration, an increase in endocrine secretion and sweat, a rise in blood pressure and body temperature, as well as muscle tension. In the short term, these changes allow us to be more focused and reactive to a threatening situation so that we can either address it or take steps to remove ourselves from it. This is commonly called the *fight or flight* scenario.

If stress continues for a prolonged period, however, we quickly hit a point of diminishing return. The results include exhaustion, hypertension, ulcers, and immune system impairment (Darley et. al., 1986). From a behavioral standpoint, an observation of any individual who is regularly *stressed out* demonstrates that the behaviors they exhibit under prolonged stress are rarely the most effective. These people are often short-tempered, make erratic and/or irrational decisions, and regularly miss important details.

While there are some people who claim they work better under stress, they're usually mistaken. If you ask people who interact with these individuals what they are like when they are stressed, you can be pretty confident that these other people's impressions will be different—and more negative. When all is said and done, stress is useful for about as long as it takes to outrun a bear. Beyond that, it is useless. For these reasons, managing stress is one of the key drivers of being able to pass our three tests for success.

When I do individual coaching, understanding what causes stress and how people behave when they are under stress is a major part of the process. One of the tools I use is the Birkman Method® personality assessment, which helps individuals identify their normal behaviors, what causes them stress, and what their stress behaviors are. One of the ways it does this is by looking at people's basic needs to develop a robust profile based on psychometrically validated scales. While it is ideal to look at this issue through a validated and reliable instrument like the Birkman Method®, you can do your own quick and dirty assessment in much the same way as we looked at our *Strengths*, *Blind Spots,* and *Areas for Improvement*.

Take out two more sheets of paper. At the top of each one, write down one of the two following sentences:

- Times when I became very stressed out

- Times when I made bad decisions because I was stressed out

Now draw a line from the top to the bottom down the center of each page. On the left-hand side of the page that reads *Times when I became very stressed out,* jot down experiences that illustrate that statement. You should have at least three to five, but it is okay to have many more. Figure 6 shows an example of what this might look like:

Times When I became stressed out	
1) Late for deadline at work	
2) Kid was sick	
3) Partner was out of town for three weeks straight	
4) Rumors were going around about lay-offs	

Figure 6. Example of Stressed List

After you have completed this task, on the right-hand side of the page, across from each stressful situation, write down one to three words that describe what could have made that situation less stressful for you. It is important to only use one to three words because more than that makes the description too situationally specific for what we are trying to do. Figure 7 provides an example of what this might look like:

Times When I became stressed out	
1) Late for deadline at work	1) Info to me on time
2) Kid was sick	2) Option to telecommute
3) Partner was out of town for three weeks straight	3) Schedule flexibility
4) Rumors were going around about lay-offs	4) More information, more often

Figure 7. Example of Stressors and Things to Cause Less Stress

After you have completed that task, take the page that reads *Times when I made bad decisions because I was stressed out.* Down the left-hand side of the page, jot down a few times when being stressed out caused you to make a bad decision. After you have done that, on the right-hand side of that page, for each situation where being stressed out caused you to make a bad decision, write down one to three words to describe what you were doing in that situation. Again, it is important to only use one to three words because more than that makes it too situationally specific.

Now that you have these pieces of paper, it is time for the big reveal. Aside from times when we are put into *fight or flight* scenarios (i.e., in danger of physical harm), stress is typically caused by not having our needs met. So, if you look down the right-hand side of the page that talks about situations where you became stressed, you may have said things like "more communication," "financial security," or "supportive boss." These are all things that you need in order to not be stressed. At this point in the game, it is not critical to determine whether these were *Sustainment* or *Values* needs, just to recognize that at these particular times, those needs were not being met.

If we look down the right-hand side of the page that talks about bad outcomes when you were stressed, it may say things like "rude to spouse," "disrespectful to boss," or "missed details." These were all suboptimal behaviors that were brought about because the physiological impacts of stress made it difficult to think straight, and much like we will learn with our

6th Assumption, they initially seemed like a good idea at the time—even if you realized half a second later you had made a mistake. The other interesting point is that if you take your *Areas for Improvement* page, there is a pretty good chance that there are clear similarities between those two lists. Once we see those similarities, it is important to take some action to make ourselves better able to handle these situations. The question, of course, is what do we do with all this information? We begin to address that with our *3rd Assumption*.

Jimmy Brown, PhD

3rd Assumption: Life Is Always in Progress

Now that we have identified *Strengths*, *Blind Spots,* and *Areas for Improvement*; you're probably asking "Okay, now what"? The answer to that question is actually quite simple— start building on your *Strengths* and addressing your *Areas for Improvement*. That may seem like a bit of an oversimplification, but the truth is, in a nutshell, that's just what you do. Of course, the execution of that simple truth is not quite so simple. But it is far from impossible.

People endeavor to improve themselves all the time, but success can be elusive. We make *New Year's resolutions*, plan *to-do lists*, and promise ourselves we will *start* or *stop* whatever we think will make a difference. The sad truth, however, is that far too often, we do not succeed in achieving these goals. We have all had the exercise equipment that gathers dust, the foreign language learning software that only gets used twice, and the art project that didn't quite get there. We then look back later and ask ourselves, "Now, why couldn't I get it together to get that done?" The answer is simply that we got too excited about the finish line and didn't worry enough about the race.

What do I mean by this? I mean that most people (myself included) tend to be outcome-oriented, but sometimes fail to be properly process-focused. We get all caught up in the cool and exciting event or result but overlook the preparation that comes before or the maintenance that comes after that event. As a result, we either don't achieve the goal or can't maintain the benefit of that outcome even after the goal is achieved. To illustrate this point, I'm going to use something I like to call the *fun wedding paradox*.

As I write this, I am of the age where most of my friends have gotten married at least once. Some of the weddings were quite solemn affairs with few attendees, little fanfare, and a sincere focus on two people committing to spend the rest of their lives together. I have also been to other weddings that were over-the-top spectacles with huge receptions and more guests than anyone could count. I have also been to some that fell somewhere in between.

A wedding is one of the clearest examples of a major life event where someone can apply their focus to many different parts of that event. In some cases, the focus of the wedding was on two people making a commitment to share their lives together and try to enrich each other in the process. In other cases, the focus of the wedding was throwing a memorable party that people would talk about for a long time. While there are exceptions to every rule, the marriages that tended to work out better focused on one particular area, while the marriages that have had issues tended to focus on an entirely different area. I will give you one guess which ones tended to result in happier and longer-lasting marriages (Hint: It was usually not the ones where there were big, fun parties).

What is the point of all this wedding talk? It illustrates that sometimes in life, we get so caught up in the excitement of some particular milestone we forget about the preparation it takes to make sure that milestone occurs correctly. We also forget about the follow-up maintenance it takes to make sure that the positive benefits from that event are maintained. This is true for everything from raising children to graduating from college, or even for something like going on a diet. We can't just decide that we want an outcome; we have to commit to the process that goes along with it. And if you really, really don't like the process, you will never ever get to the goal. For these reasons, the focus of this chapter is on providing a framework for developing the habits that build on insights we gained during the exercises described during the discussion of our *2nd Assumption*. This framework enables us to create the habits that help us build on our strengths, and either address or minimize the impact of our opportunities for improvement.

There are multiple definitions associated with the noun "habit." The two that are relevant here relate to a "pattern of action that is acquired and has become so automatic that it is difficult to break," or "a tendency to perform a certain action or behave in a certain way" (Webster's, 1996). Habits are the things we do day in and day out that form the patterns of our lives. They tend to develop over time and always require some degree of decision making to develop, as well as some degree of decision making to discontinue. Good habits are the ones that promote outcomes that lead to happy and health lives, whereas bad habits are the ones that lead to unhappy and unhealthy lives.

All this sounds simple enough, but here is the irony… good habits tend to require significant effort to pick up and are very easy to break. Bad habits, however, tend to be very easy to start and tend to be very hard to break. Why is that? I once heard a friend who was trying to quit smoking claim that it had something to do with God having a sense of humor. While that may or may not be the case, the real driver of this paradox may have to do with when the benefits of those habits are initially experienced by each individual.

Good habits are good habits because they have significant long-term benefits. For example, starting and staying on a regular exercise program can reduce stress, increase cardiovascular strength and often leads to a longer and healthier life. Initially, however, good habits tend to have very small short-term benefits and even some short-term detriments. That new exercise program may not make you feel that great when you first start. If you have not exercised in a while, it may make you feel tired and sore, and even cause you to walk funny because you are using muscles you actually forgot you had. While you logically *know* that keeping with the program will be beneficial in the long run, if it hurts too much to keep going, many people will have no trouble finding excuses to discontinue the process. Moreover, the fact that if you take just a few days off and get used to not having to maintain the discipline required to keep that healthy regime, that inactivity can become a habit—more easily formed than the hard work of exercising.

Bad habits, on the other hand, are bad because they can be detrimental in the long term. Ironically, every bad habit initially has some short-term benefit. For example, smoking cigarettes has been linked to numerous terminal diseases, costs significant amounts of money over a lifetime, and may require one to stand outside in bad weather just to smoke. Why, then, do people ever pick up smoking? While I have never been a smoker myself, my understanding is that it is relaxing and enjoyable, and the calming effect of nicotine seems to provide the perception of a positive impact. That impact, however, also leads to a nicotine dependence that can make quitting especially difficult, even when the person realizes that they should do so. The amount of difficulty people have quitting smoking can be illustrated by the number of products available for those who are trying to break the habit. Finding exact numbers on what Americans spend on smoking cessation is not easy, but I have seen unreviewed sources put the amount as anywhere from $263 million a year and up.

Drawing from these two examples illustrates the two key points about habits. Bad habits are easy to acquire and hard to break. Conversely, good habits tend to be hard to acquire and easy to break. Recognizing this, the question invariably comes up of how to develop the good habits and then break the bad ones. That question is pretty much the crux of this chapter.

A key component of developing good habits is to not merely focus on the outcome, but to commit to the process. I'm sure some people reading this are now saying something like, "I thought we were supposed to start with the end in mind?" After all, Steven Covey says so (Covey, 2004), and many success coaches get very wrapped up in being *outcome driven.* Moreover, we must have a clear vision of the end to be able to determine what the appropriate steps are to reach that end (i.e., the process). Where many people make a mistake, however, is focusing solely on the outcome and forgetting about all the steps that have to take place to achieve that outcome. So how is this done? By following a fairly straight forward process…

- First, define the goal.
- Second, determine the steps necessary to achieve that goal.
- Third, identify the behaviors required to execute those steps.
- Fourth, identify progress checks along the way.
- Fifth, force yourself to begin performing those steps (and keep doing them until they become habits).
- Sixth, don't stop doing them until the goal is achieved.

Some people read through this process and feel like it is some great new insight and become a bit intimidated by it. They think that it requires a great deal of focus to not only learn the new habits they need to be successful, but to also learn the process of developing those habits. To be honest, experience suggests that people are often more intimidated by the prospect of learning the process of developing new habits than they are of the new habits themselves. And if we think about this as something we've never done before, it can be a bit intimidating. To overcome this, we have to realize we have all done things like this before and get past that unnecessary intimidation.

One of the ways to reduce the intimidation factor of a process like this is to adopt some kind of structured approach to that effort. While there are lots of crazy, expensive classes out there on things like goal setting and execution, I'd recommend starting off with something simpler like the worksheet illustrated in Figure 8:

Goal:
Step 1:
Step 2:
Step 3:
Step 4:
Step 5:
Behavioral changes I need to make to take those steps:
Progress Checks:

Figure 8. **Goal Setting Worksheet**

Yes, this worksheet does look overly simplistic, but that's the point. When we accept that life is always in progress, we have to also accept that we want to reduce complexity and confusion. We want to embrace Occam's Razor, which holds that all things being equal, the simplest solution is always the best. Sure, we could make this all kinds of complicated with fancy terms and methods, but why do that? Focus on what really matters. Focus on developing the habits to reach your goals.

Let's say we wanted to use this worksheet to save up enough money to have a down payment on a house. Sure, you can go read any of the dozens of books that talk about savings plans and compounded interest and rates of return. Or you could just make something like Figure 9:

Goal: Save for down payment on a house

Step 1: Determine house much house I can afford

Step 2: Calculate much down payment I would need

Step 3: Identify where I can cut costs to put more money back

Step 4: Set up new interest baring savings account just for house

Step 5: Set up autodraft to move money into account before I spend it on other stuff

Behavioral changes I need to make to take those steps:
a) Only eat out one night a week rather than 4
b) Get rid of cable TV and only use antenna or web app television
c) Cancel fancy gym membership and use free gym at office

Progress Checks:
a) Check spending once a month
b) Check savings account balance once a month

Figure 9. Example of Goal Setting Worksheet

Obviously, this is not an overly complicated process. It is just a matter of figuring out what matters and taking steps to get there. It is also important to remember to write things like this down, as that seems to make these commitments more real and we tend to hold ourselves more accountable for our actions. It also helps us come back on track when we slip up. For example, in our home down payment savings example, this person may have some weeks where they go out to dinner way more than the one time they promised themselves. That is okay because *things are in process* and having it written down like this helps that setback be a bump in the road rather than a permanent distraction. It also helps us focus on the fundamentals of our goal. Focusing on fundamentals is critical, and many of us have been doing this since we were little kids—we just didn't realize it.

****

As children, many people were involved in some kind of extracurricular activity at some point in time. It could be music, it could be dance, or it could be sports. For some people, it is a combination of all of the above and then some. Some people stick with just one thing the whole way through, while other people tried a lot of different things. Some people were highly successful, some just had a good time. Others may have gotten frustrated and begged their parents to be allowed to quit.

Regardless of the activity or the desired outcome, most of our lessons and practices did not start off focusing on the desired outcome (e.g., performing a song or competing in a game). Instead they focused on repetition of rudimentary fundamentals to develop the particular skills that would lead to the desired outcomes (e.g., playing scales or running drills). I myself was not a huge fan of those basic activities. Like many children, I thought they were boring and really didn't see the point. Looking back on those experiences, however, those individuals who embraced learning the fundamental skills were the ones who were the most successful when it came time to put them together to achieve the desired outcome. Why? Because being successful at such activities requires us to not only become proficient in those particular skills, but it also requires us to have the mechanics of those skills habituated to the point where we don't have to think about all the individual steps that go into those activities.

This is not to say that we can only learn new skills and habits as children. Despite the saying about old dogs and new tricks, it is never too late. We can begin at any age. Take marathon runners, for example. According to some sources, less than 0.5% of the U.S. population has ever completed a marathon (Statistic Brain Research Institute, 2016). Even fewer run them regularly. Most people who do run marathons do not start until they reach adulthood—some until later adulthood (my father didn't start until his mid-60s). Quite a few people who decide to attempt to run a marathon do not succeed. Why? Because they are only focused on the run rather than developing the habits and lifestyle that enable them to run 26.2 miles in one shot.

Go onto Google and search for a local marathon. Not the Boston or New York marathons that require qualifying and offer big prize money, but the hundreds of local marathons in which anyone can just sign up and participate. With very few exceptions, each of those local marathons will have a link to a recommended training program or links to local running clubs with their own training programs. Some groups are very seriously competitive, whereas others are more about offering moral support and education for novice runners about how to have fun and not get hurt. Despite those differences, the commonalities among all these training programs is that they all start six to seven months before the actual event, and *none* of them start off expecting someone to run 26.2 miles on the first day. In some cases, the first run of the training schedule is as little as 1½ miles. Over the next six to seven months the schedules build up to where each runner gradually gets into better and better shape and becomes more and more confident that they can complete the task. This is not unlike Jeff Olsen's

Slight Edge approach where he recommends taking small initial steps and building over time toward the desired result (2011).

This idea of taking small steps and building on them over time to progress toward the goals we want is a key part of the habit-building approach of our *3rd Assumption*. We have to take small, concerted steps to instill the habits we need. Tired of having a messy house? Start by deciding you're going to make your bed every day. Want to learn a new language? You could sign up for some expensive immersion classes, but maybe it would be better to download some $2.99 app onto your tablet and try using that for 15 minutes a day, four times a week. Want to remember to talk slowly so that others can understand you when you get excited (something I work on constantly)? Start off each day by writing down five times *I will talk slowly* onto a piece of paper. It sounds like a small little thing, but these simple habit-building exercises do work... if you stick with them.

We have to remember, however, that changing habits doesn't always work in a linear process. To be honest, I've never seen it go that way, and anyone who has claimed they did do it as a linear process usually starts to change their story once you drill down into details. We're going to have missteps, we're going to make mistakes, and we're going to have to course-correct along the way. The thing to remember is to get up, dust yourself off, and course-correct as soon as possible. The reason why this is so important can be illustrated through simple geometry.

****

Even though we have established that real-life improvement and changing habits is almost never a linear process, let's pretend temporarily that it could be. Now let's imagine that we know *where we are,* and we know *where we want to be.* Now let's imagine that our path from here to there is a straight line. We could draw a picture that looks something like Figure 10.

Figure 10. Path to Our Goal

This conceptualization could be anything from buying a new car, to becoming a lawyer, to learning to paint. It doesn't matter what you're trying to do; we just have to recognize that there is a path that must be taken from here to there. We have to start down this road knowing that things will come along that may try to knock us off our path. Some may be bad luck. Some may be bad people. Some may be decisions that didn't work out the way we planned (more on that in our *6th Assumption*). Regardless of the cause, there will be little detours along the way. The important thing about these little detours is to remember that when we encounter them, we simply need to course-correct and get back on track. Doing this might look something like Figure 11:

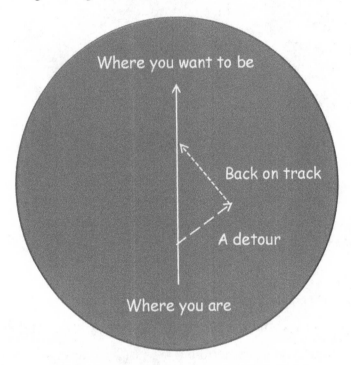

Figure 11. Detour and Course Correction

These little detours are common in life. What's key is recognizing is that the longer it takes to course-correct, the longer it takes to get back on track toward where we want to be. My personal journey to complete my educational goals is a perfect example of that. When I was in college, I learned about this thing called Industrial and Organizational Psychology. I decided that that was what I wanted to do, even though you need at least a master's degree to get most jobs in the field, and a PhD to really progress in that career. Moreover, admittance to those graduate programs is atypically competitive. Despite the odds, I managed to get admitted to what was then one of the better master's programs in the country, and my plan was go straight through and finish my doctorate.

Despite this clear line of sight between where I was and where I wanted to be, things did not quite go as planned. Due to a variety of reasons, I was not able to go directly from the master's to the doctoral program at the school I was attending like I had planned. There were a couple of avenues where I could have gone directly into a doctoral program at another school, but I decided I would take a break for a couple of years before going back. A couple turned into five, and five turned into eight before I was finally reenrolled in a doctoral program and returned to progressing toward my goal.

There were several points along the way where I could have course-corrected much sooner and made my journey much shorter. The main reason I didn't was because I let myself get temporarily distracted from my goal. I let other momentary priorities take precedence over my long-term goal. Instead of progressing like something we see in Figure 10 or Figure 11, my path was more like Figure 12:

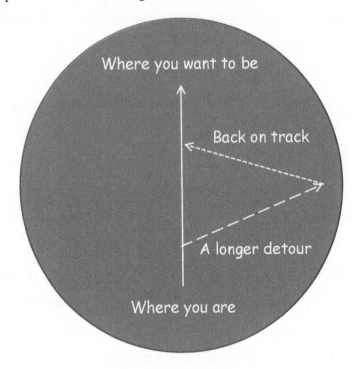

Figure 12. Longer Course Correction

Obviously, my *back on track* trip was longer than I had wanted it to be. The great irony of this example is that I faced some trials in the early 2000s that led me to realize how important it was to go back and finish my training—and those situations would have been much less challenging if I had just stayed focused on my original goal. The good news, though, is that coming out of that experience gave me more insight into how important it is to recognize that our lives will always have ups and downs, and how we manage those has a huge impact our success and happiness. Managing those ups and downs is the focus of our next assumption.

4th Assumption: You Are Going to Have Ups and Downs

There are a lot of self-help books out there about the ups. For example, *The Happiness Advantage* advocates focusing primarily on the ups as the best way to be healthy and successful (Achor, 2010). It draws heavily from the positive psychology movement, which takes a strengths-based approach to mental and emotional wellbeing. This approach is a vast improvement over the previously prevailing therapeutic approaches that simply dwelled on what is *wrong* with a person. That approach could cause what is often referred to as a downward spiral, where a person becomes so focused on what is going wrong in their lives that they forget to appreciate what is going right. The bads are reinforced, the goods are overlooked. If we don't appreciate the positives in our lives, we will have a very hard time becoming and staying successful and happy.

This does not mean, however, that we can just go around being Pollyannas. Absolutely not, because the simple truth is that life does not always go as planned. In fact, if you ever meet a person who claims their life only has ups, I would recommend being very cautious around them. They are either lying, delusional, or are the single luckiest person who ever lived. And if they have been that phenomenally lucky up to this point, statistically their luck is due to run out. Personally, I don't know if I want to be around when that happens because the collateral damage might be spectacular.

Apart from avoiding said collateral damage, there is no shame in admitting that you have down times. Everyone has them. Even the most successful people you've ever heard of. Grab any biography of any famous person and they'll talk about the lean years they had before success and how important those were in forming who they are as a person. Why do they always spend so much time on this? Because one of the key differences between successful and unsuccessful people is that successful people recognize that the most important thing about getting knocked down is getting back up.

I used to work for a very senior consulting executive who was well known for saying things along the lines of "I don't have any problems. I have some challenges, and I have a lot of annoyances. But I don't really have any problems." This comment intrigued me because my initial thought was, "Sure, you don't have many problems. You're a bigwig here and make close to a million dollars a year." It is a lot easier to not have problems when you can *afford* to pay someone to take care of them for you!

As time went on, however, I learned that she had an extremely colorful past. This included starting out as a waitress in a seedy dinner to pay for college, being one of the first female managers in a very male-dominated firm and having to hold her own against some pretty extreme harassment. One of the attributes that led to her being able to rise through the ranks despite the "old boy network" was her demonstration that she could work through the various challenges that inevitably came up and keep moving forward. Obviously, she operated from an assumption that objectionable things would happen, but she could work through them.

Of course, this individual was only one example among many. Oprah Winfrey was fired from her first job in television and told she was "unfit for TV." Michael Jordan was famously cut from his high school basketball team. The late Steve Jobs was fired from his own company (i.e., Apple) before he came back and led the design of the now ubiquitous iPhones and iPads. We could continue this list for quite some time, but you get the point. As we look at all those examples, however, it becomes apparent that one of the key tools that successful people use to manage these issues is to categorize them in a way that makes them seem less like permanent roadblocks and more like learning experiences. While there are a lot of different ways to slice and dice this concept, for our discussion we'll divide these challenges into three main categories:

- *Falling Down*: Something that gets in your way because you made a mistake
- *Speed Bumps*: Something that gets in your way because of someone or something else
- *Failure:* Something that gets in your way and you let it keep you down

It is inevitable that each of us could have any of these experiences at different points in our lives. It is less a question of *if*, but *when*. Of course, the real question is: When these things *do* occur, how do we handle them?

When we *Fall Down*, we simply fix it, learn from it, and then move on. When we hit *Speed Bumps*, we should accept that the issue is not our fault and figure out ways to avoid the same challenges in the future. When we have a *Failure*… the truth is, we only fail when we stop getting back up. If we understand that these things are going to happen, and we can work through them, then we will get up and will never actually fail.

There is an abundance of stories of people who had downs but never failed. Walt Disney was fired by the *Kansas City Star* newspaper in 1919 because he "lacked imagination." J. K. Rowling was rejected by multiple publishers before she found one who was willing to take a chance on a book about a boy wizard. While Ted Turner grew up in a relatively well-off family, his father was abusive, and he had to take over the family business after his father committed suicide while Turner was still in college. Again, these are just a few of the countless examples.

All of these stories have several important commonalities. The first is that the people involved became very successful despite challenges that would make some people give up. The second is that *they did not give up*. Pretty much all of them admit that they wanted to, but somehow found a way not to. The third is that when people talk about these individuals' success, they often forget about all the effort that went into creating these positive outcomes.

This is not unlike one of my favorite stories from Tony Robbins's *Awaken the Giant Within* about the stonecutter who walks up to a giant boulder and splits it in half with a blow of a hammer (2003). Everyone who sees this is amazed and thinks that this man has done an amazing thing. They feel it is some magical feat of strength or luck. What they don't realize is that this man has been walking up to this boulder and hitting in the exact same spot every day for a very long time. And while Robbins doesn't identify the exact number of times that the man had to come up to the boulder, he does say it was probably more than 1,004. Given that, it would not be surprising if the full story of this man and the rock showed that he tripped a few times during all his walks up to it. Maybe he had various distractions get in his way. Maybe he even dropped the hammer on his toe a few times going back and forth from that boulder. And if the man had a family, I'm sure they asked him more than once why he kept going and hitting that big old rock. Despite all that, he kept getting up, stuck to his task, and accomplished an amazing thing in the end.

Here's the other thing about the boulder story that isn't covered in Robbins's book that maybe should be… As great as this accomplishment was, I'm sure there were times after this where the man who did it felt he wasn't that great. He probably even questioned why he kept going back to hit that boulder day after day. I suspect that more than once, he thought about giving up.

I say this because we all have those days when we don't feel successful. It is perfectly natural and normal. Many of the greatest scientists and artists in history have been their own worst critics. We can look brilliant musicians like Axl Rose and Kurt Cobain, who are well known for being overly critical of their own work. Patrick Henry Bruce was considered one of the great painters of the early twentieth century, but he was so self-critical that he destroyed most of his own work (Agee, 1979). Even when everyone tells them that they are great, these people think they could and *should* be better. This is what drives them reach new levels and create new things. The difference between those who self-destruct and those who keep creating is that the successful ones don't let those down times hold them back. If anything, those who continue to succeed use the passion developed from the pain of the down times to drive them in the up times to be the best they can.

****

Plato is credited with saying that the unexamined life is not worth living. And to some degree, we all know this. This is why it isn't just brilliant scientists and artists who are challenged with self-doubt and second guessing—it is anyone who has the drive to be happy and successful. No matter how well we are doing, if we look hard enough, we will find someone who *appears* to be doing better than we are. If we focus too much on this, we end up feeling worse about our own state, regardless of how well we are doing. The irony, of course, is that there is likely someone, somewhere envying each of us in that same way. And given that we don't know what is going on behind the scenes of those who *appear* to be doing better, it may be one of the people we are admiring!

What is the point of all this? Simply that the most important thing we can do is to learn to get back up when we get knocked down, and not stress out about whether we are doing better or worse than someone else. Does it really matter? Can it really be learned? The answer to both of those questions is a resounding yes!

To illustrate this point, I'm going to share some information about my high school days. I went to an all-boys Catholic high school. My family wasn't Catholic, but it was the best high school in the city at the time. It was challenging to get in due to the competitive admission process, and a financial struggle for my family to pay the tuition, but my parents made the investment because they saw the value for me in this experience. While the school had a strong focus on academics, there was an even stronger focus on learning to be good men and to manage life. The principal of the school was a priest named Fr. George Tribou who would bring all the freshmen parents in every year and basically rip them apart for taking care of everything for us and not letting us learn how to get back up once we fell down. In fact, he guaranteed that during each student's time at his school, they would not succeed at something, if for no other reason than so that we could learn to get back up. He also had a favorite saying: he didn't care how many doctors and lawyers he produced, he only cared about how many good husbands and fathers. It was very particular system that carries on to this day, long after Father had passed.

Does this system work? While I won't way that everyone who came through that system was successful (using the standard we defined in our *1st Assumption*), I will say that upwards of 90% of the students from that school go on to college, and at least 20% of my senior class now holds a law degree, a medical degree, or a PhD. That is more than 10 times the rate of those credentials in the general population average. By any method of statistical calculation, that is way more than can be expected by pure chance. Looking at this from a behavior science standpoint, once we eliminate random chance as a possible driver of the outcome, we can consider that something unique is likely the determinant of this outcome. In this case, that determinant appears to be a common experience of learning how to get back up when we hit bumps in the road.

Those bumps in the road are going to happen. There is no avoiding it; we simply have to accept them and move forward. The task of *accepting* that you're going have challenges and then determining the perspective that we apply to those challenges is a big part of what allows us to manage them in appropriate and effective way.

Appropriately managing challenges consists of two key activities. The first activity is making sure we do not freak out. As we discussed earlier, ongoing stress causes us to start engaging in our least effective behaviors when new challenges pop up. If we have gone into the process accepting that something imperfect might happen, whatever occurs should not be too much of a surprise. Unfortunately, many people do not do this. Those who do go in accepting that there may be challenges usually perform better.

To illustrate this point, I'll share an experience from several years ago when I was working with a large consulting firm. We were integrating the IT infrastructure of several acquired firms for a major insurance company. It was a *huge* job. There were lots of people involved (the consulting team alone comprised more than 200 people across the U.S., plus the offshore team), lots of different teams, and a whole lot of things that could (and did) not go as planned.

My team was tasked with designing how we would manage the performance measurement capability of this new merged organization. This meant that we made the decisions about how we were going to measure, track, and report the outcomes of each unit within this new organization. Our deliverables would impact every part of the organization, so we had a lot visibility. As such, my own role also had a lot of visibility.

This project occurred at a time in my career when I was just starting to think about some of the concepts in this book. I was also just starting to play around with some of the ideas we are discussing here. As such, one of the first rules that I put in place for my team was that we would *accept* that there were things that were probably not going to go as planned. We would also *accept* that other people on the project would likely freak out about those things—but within our team, we would *choose* to stay calm, focus on the issue, and keep moving forward. Luckily, I had a team that was willing to indulge my experimentation with such a novel approach, so putting these rules into practice was not as difficult as it could have been. In the end, this team was not only atypically effective, but much more effective than I would have predicted. Thus, we stuck with this plan.

What was most surprising, however, was that a couple months into the effort, my boss called me into her office to discuss some concerns one of the senior partners had expressed about me and my team. While this senior partner was perfectly happy with our outputs and the quality of our work, he was very concerned that we just didn't seem stressed enough. He thought maybe something was wrong and it was making *him* nervous.

To understand this strange worry, we have to set the context. There are some parts of the consulting world where looking like you are stressed out is actually part of the culture. This particular firm was one of those places, and my team and I were violating that norm. While my boss and I did have a nice chuckle over the irony of this guy getting nervous because we were not, it did require me to explain to him what was going on. After I listened to his initial coaching, he and I had a quick chat about stress, some of its physical and psychological impacts, why I had put those rules in place, and that my team was the only one that was ahead of schedule.

After I shared this information, this senior partner sat there for what seemed like an eternity, staring at me in silence. For a minute, I thought he might be trying to decide if he should fire me. In fact, this was the one time on this project where I let myself get truly nervous. To be honest, if it hadn't had been for some pretty intense sales training very early in my career about when not to talk, I probably would have opened my mouth and made things worse. Luckily, it had been pretty well ingrained into me that in situations like that, the best thing to do was sit there quietly and let him think.

Suddenly, he shrugged his shoulders, said he was okay with what we were doing, and told me to keep up the good work. In fact, he never questioned me about any of my decisions again. He later become one of my biggest advocates. The issue in this particular situation was not the quality of work, but the concern that our lack of stress was an indicator of a lack of focus. A lack of focus usually translates to a lack of effort, which could lead to something happening that could be a problem later. Concern about what could happen later was what was causing him unwarranted stress. Helping him realize that our lack of stress helped us stay *more* focused managed and removed his stress. And how we manage stress leads to our next point about how we deal with challenges.

In addition to not freaking out when challenges occur, we also have to not spend all our time focused on things that *might* occur but have not yet. Does this mean we don't think through possible outcomes? Of course not! Does it mean that we don't take action to reduce the risk of those occurring, and have a plan in case they do? Most definitely not. What it does mean, however, is that once we have done that risk assessment and put our mitigation plans in place, we move forward with confidence that we have taken all the reasonable steps we can to deal with it and focus on the most positive possible outcome.

To help drive this point home I will share an extremely personal story about my daughter. Like any proud parent, I could easily go on for pages about how great she is and how many wonderful things she does. But I'm not going to do that. What I am going to do is share with you that she did not start regularly sleeping through the night until she was nearly two years old! When I share this story in live sessions, it's easy to pick out the parents in the room based on their reaction to that statement. The parents are ones who look at me with a combined expression of horror and sympathy. For the rest of the crowd, I have to explain that statement's significance.

For those who are not parents, or who were lucky enough to have children who were good sleepers, most children go through some period of time where they don't sleep through the night. They will wake up at random times and refuse to go back to sleep. The parents usually take turns waking up to take care of the baby and become very tired and frustrated with each other. For many children, like my son, this phase only lasts a month or two. For a few children, like my daughter, it lasts much longer. We experienced nearly two years of being woken up almost every night, after anywhere from 10 minutes to three hours, by a wailing child whom nothing would calm down. And even if she did stop crying, she didn't go back to sleep—she wanted you to play with her. Otherwise she'd go back to wailing. You never knew what time it was coming. You weren't completely sure if it *was* coming. You did know, however, that there was a pretty good chance that the six to eight hours of rest you wanted to get that night could be quickly cut in half.

This was a very rough period for my wife and myself. And it was made more challenging by the fact that we each handled it quite differently. Going to bed, we both knew there was a pretty good chance we were going to get woken up at some point. My wife's stress management approach was to put a lot of thought into the situation. She would think about whether our daughter was going to wake up and what she would do if that happened. As a result, even on the precious few nights when our daughter did not wake up, my wife still could not get a good night's sleep because she was thinking about what to do if it happened. While part of this is maternal instinct, part of it was also just her personal style.

While I went to bed with the same knowledge, I was very focused on making sure that I got to sleep as quickly as possible because I knew I needed to get my sleep in when I could. I did this because I knew I could not control which nights our daughter did and did not wake up. All I could control was how I behaved before she woke up, while she was awake, and after she finally fell back to sleep. On nights when our daughter woke up, I still didn't get as much sleep as I wanted to, but I got much more than I would have had I been lying awake worried. On those rare nights when our daughter did manage to sleep through the whole night, I managed to get a full night's sleep.

Does this mean that my approach was *right,* and my wife's approach was *wrong*? As a husband, I feel obligated to say absolutely not, because we are just very different people and approach things in different ways. As a husband, I'm also obligated to say that my wife is perfect and can do no wrong, because that is what good husbands do. As a consultant and coach, however, I do have to point out that during this trying time, one of us got much more sleep than the other (and these different answers are a perfect example of our discussion from our *2nd Assumption* about how we all have different roles at different times). A key part of my perspective that led to me being able to handle this situation differently came from my experience as a consultant and a coach, where I've learned that there is always going to be something less than ideal going on in life. How we manage those surprises is a key contributor to our success.

One of the things we do on big consulting projects to manage these unpleasant occurrences is using something called a Risk Assessment Tool (sometimes jokingly called a R.A.T.). If you've ever been involved in any kind of big project at work (e.g., IT, construction, logistics), you've probably been exposed to something like this. It is basically the process of thinking through and documenting any potential negative occurrence that could affect the scope, schedule, or cost of a project, and then coming up with some way to mitigate those things that are potentially major impacts. Under normal circumstances, these risks and issues are captured in some kind of matrix or spreadsheet and then assigned weights based upon the likelihood of something occurring, and the severity of the impact if it does occur. Weights are usually numbers that can be used to calculate and rank the overall importance of each risk and issue. The various possibilities are then discussed in meetings (sometimes for hours on end) and managed accordingly.

In theory, it is all supposed to be a very neat and formal process that allows us to actively manage these issues rather than dwelling or ruminating, or letting things slip until we can't ignore them anymore. The truth, however, is that it is much messier than it is supposed to be. I've seen a lot of project managers who spend a ton of time overmanaging the smallest risks and driving those around them nuts. Despite these misapplications, though, there are lessons to be learned from this approach that we can apply to our personal lives. In fact, this process is probably even *more* powerful for our personal lives because we only have to worry about ourselves and those individuals we directly interact with, rather than a team of 75-plus people across three different countries. We just have to follow a few simple steps.

The first step is developing a personal risk/issue inventory. Please remember that the goal of this inventory is not to give us more to worry about or to make us more stressed. The goal to help us identify and document the things we need to keep an eye on so that we can keep track of them, or better yet, realize they aren't that big a deal after all.

To do this, take out another piece of paper and put the following headings at the top: *Risk/Issue, Chance, Impact, Did What I Can Do?* Then draw lines from top to bottom. When you're done, it should look something like Figure 13.

Risk/Issue	Chance	Impact	Did what I can do?

Figure 13. Sample Risk and Issues Log

Once this is done, we simply populate this with somewhere between three and seven of the biggest and/or most common risks/issues we have to deal with in our daily lives. These could be things that aren't very common but if they happen, it would be catastrophic, so we want to mitigate. Or they could be little things we have to deal with every single day, but not keeping them in perspective will create stress for us. It might also be helpful to think back to our *1st Assumption* and consider our *Sustainment* and *Values* needs, as those are often closely related to our personal risks.

For each of these, assess the *Chance* of it occurring as High, Medium, or Low, and the potential *Impact* won you as High, Medium, or Low. *Did What I Can Do?* is where we note whether we have taken any action to address this issue, and if so, what. It is simply a place for us to take stock of how we might manage these challenges. Figure 14 shows an example of what one of these lists might look like when populated.

Risk/Issue	Chance	Impact	Did what I can do?
1) Heart Attack – Some family history	Low	High	Yes- Eat right & exercise
2) Potential layoff from work – rumors floating around office	Med.	High	Yes- Doing job well. Net-working just in case
3) Middle kid will throw temper tantrum	High	Low	Yes – Told them not to, Will ignore them when they do
4) May get kidnapped by aliens – Youngest kid worried about it	Low	Low	No – But am wearing "anti-alien bracelet"

Figure 14. Example of Personal Risk/Issue Inventory

Obviously, things like health issues and job risks are among of the most common concerns for working adults. They are also the ones that can have the greatest impacts. Luckily, they are also the ones we have the most control over. Sure, we can't completely control our genetics or whether we end up on the wrong side of some accountant's spreadsheet, but we *can* control how we plan for them, mitigate them, and react to them. That is the whole point of an exercise like this: helping us realize that these risks are manageable. Once we do, the stress from them decreases so that we can focus on making sure we are meeting our needs in a way that is consistent with what we value.

5th Assumption: No Person Is an Island

In 1624, English poet John Donne published his *Meditation XVII,* which included the now-famous line "No man is an island, entire of itself; every man is a piece of the continent, a part of the main." While literature professors can spend hours deliberating on the various interpretations of this prose, the long and short of it is that we are not alone in this world and we must learn to effectively interact with other people and in our environment if we want to be happy and successful. If we fail to understand that, we can find ourselves in some serious trouble. Not only are we dependent on other people for division of labor and acquisition of necessary resources, but also for our psychological wellbeing (Wohn, Peng, & Zytko, 2017). While there may be a few people out there who are better off when left alone, most of us need some sort of social interaction to remain sane.

Much of our understanding of how we interact with others comes from what psychologists call "ecological systems theory." This is an idea first popularized by Urie Bronfenbrenner, who saw an individual's development as being critically shaped by his or her environment (1979). Our experiences in the world, and particularly with other people, have a massive effect on how we develop and grow. While this is related to the discussion we had with our *2nd Assumption* about how we will become our parents whether we like it or not, this is a much broader approach in that we are not just dealing with how we became who we are—we are dealing with what we do today and in the future. Moreover, this theory takes into account not just our parental figures, but all the people that we interact with, as well as other environmental factors.

How do we understand our ecosystem? First, we need to understand what a system is. One of the best ways to conceptualize this is basic systems theory. There are a lot of different definitions out there, but when we take them as a whole, they tend to come down to a system being an interconnected set of activities and attributes that drive toward some goal. The goal of a biological system is to grow and reproduce. The goal of a computer system is to calculate and produce data. The goal of theological system is to provide a structured set of beliefs that helps people manage their lives. For our discussion, the goal is for you to have a happy and successful life. Given that, we have to ask what system (or, more to the point, systems) come into play.

The answer to that question can be a bit tricky, because as we examined in our discussion of our *1st Assumption*, what we need to be happy and successful is unique to each person, and those needs may change as we go through different stages of our lives. Moreover, as we discussed with our *2nd Assumption*, we all play different roles at different times, which means the systems we interact with also change. As such, the systems we are a part of constantly shift, and the strategies we use to manage them must be flexible enough to also evolve as needed.

Some people may get a little confused and nervous when they first consider this concept. That is perfectly understandable—it can initially seem a bit complicated and overwhelming. But don't let yourself get nervous, because this concept is kind of like one of those crazy Magic Eye posters from the early 1990s where you can't tell what is going on until you relax your perspective and just go with it. Once we do that, we can learn to differentiate between what system inputs we should take action on, and what is just noise.

To begin developing this understanding, we will turn to Stephen Covey's work on *The 7 Habits of Highly Effective People*. If you're reading this book, you probably already have an interest in self-improvement and have likely at least heard of

Stephen Covey, and maybe even read this or another one of his books. For those who haven't, the *7 Habits* has been one of the most popular self-help texts for more than 25 years and has reached the point where it is so ensconced in business lexicon that it constantly gets misquoted by people who claim to have read it…but actually haven't. It is also one of the reasons I tried to prevent this book from having seven constructs, but as we discussed earlier, things did not work out that way—a slight *speed bump*, you might say!

One of the more interesting concepts that Covey discusses in his book is our Circle of Influence vs. our Circle of Concern (Covey, 2004). Covey sees our Circle of Concern as anything where we have some degree of mental or emotional involvement. This can include things we are directly related to, such as our health and our children, as well as things we have less control over, such as the national debt and the risk of nuclear war. For those of us who are prone to stress, that circle can get pretty big.

The Circle of Influence includes things within our Circle of Concern that we can actual *do* something about. For example, we can proactively affect our health and how our children are raised, so those would be within our Circle of Influence. Most of us, however, don't have much direct impact on things like the national debt or the risk of nuclear war, so those would not be within our Circle of Influence. Covey recommends using positive energies to expand our Circle of Influence so that it gets wider and wider. Figure 15 illustrates this.

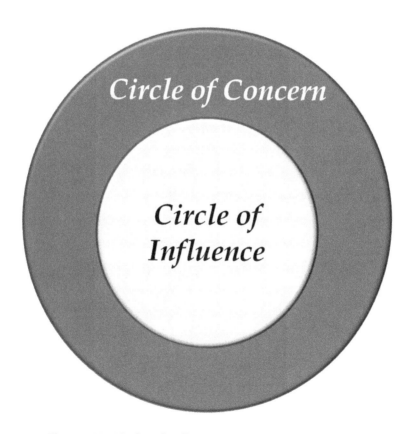

Figure 15. Circle of Influence and Circle of Concern

Using positive energy to expand that Circle of Influence sounds like a neat idea, but to be honest, it may not be realistic. First, each of us only has a finite amount of time and effort. As such, the more we expand that circle, the less we can focus on each of the individual things we keep adding to it. Second, while there are lots of evolving methods related to positive psychology and change methods such as Appreciative Inquiry that focus on these positive ontologies, they are all focused on positive applications to what we are currently doing—not on using those positive energies to expand our impact. As such, it is hard to find clear guidance on how to do this.

In addition to a lack of clarity about what steps need to be taken to achieve this objective, none of the notes that I took over the years, nor any of the people that I formally interviewed for this book ever talked about anything that even remotely sounded like proactively working on expanding their Circle of Influence. In fact, most of the successful and happy people that I have met over the years were acutely aware that there is only so much that one person can realistically do. While being willing to take on more risks and more responsibility is an important part of moving up the corporate ladder, being smart about what you do and how you do it is just as, if not even more, important.

How exactly does this work? Much like we did with Maslow's Hierarchy back in our *1st Assumption*, we have to take Covey's idea of the circles and tweak it to make it more realistic and actionable. We have to figure out where we should *Listen*, where we should *Lead*, and what we can actively *Manage*. We also have to determine what we are simply not going to worry about because it is noise. These differentiations are important for two reasons. The first reason is that, as our *5th Assumption* clearly states, no person is an island, and we have to interact with other people in some form or another to be successful. The second reason is that to be successful and happy, we have to learn to work through other people.

Apart from a few creative artists who can lock themselves in a room and paint some masterpiece, pretty much no one becomes successful on their own. Any entrepreneur who has grown a company from a garage to an industry leader will expound on the importance of finding the right people. The reason for this is that when we work as individuals, our ability to contribute is limited to our own individual efforts. When we learn to work through others, those limits disappear because we can have multiple people working on multiple things at the same time. We multiply our outcomes and our contribution as we multiply the members of our environment we are able to work through. I know this sounds kind of like the pitch for a lot of direct marketing companies (e.g. Amway) that try to get you to recruit your friends into your downline, but that's because, well, it sort of is. The way we become more effective and successful is to learn how to coordinate our efforts through others to achieve bigger and bigger goals.

How does one learn to work through others? First, we must determine what we can *Manage*. These are things and people that we can directly influence ourselves. Next, we have to determine what we can *Lead*. These are the things and people that we can indirectly influence, but we do so based on how we *Manage* and influence other people. Then we have to identify the people and things we should *Listen* to. These are the people and things we do not have any direct or indirect influence over, but need to keep a bead on because their influence and actions may affect someone or something that we are responsible for. The rest is just plain old noise. Figure 16 illustrates this.

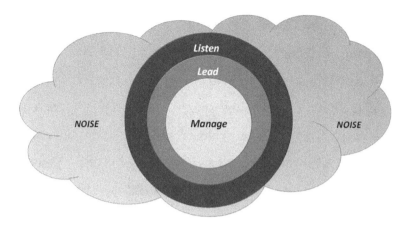

Figure 16. Listen, Lead, and Manage

One important consideration when figuring out what you can actually *Manage* is to remember that most people can only directly manage five to nine things in any given environment at any given time. Why five to nine, you ask? This goes back to early work on memory and processing that showed that the average person could best process large amounts of information by breaking it down into chunks of data of quantities of seven, plus or minus two (Miller, 1956). Coincidentally, this why local phone numbers in the U.S. are seven digits. Of course, with so many large metropolitan areas going to 10-digit, dialing like this has kind of gone out the window, but everyone has smartphones these days, so it's no longer necessary to memorize a lot of seven-digit numbers.

So, how does this apply to our understanding of *Managing, Leading,* and *Listening*? Using this logic, we can surmise that most *effective* manager will only have between five and nine *direct* reports at any one time. Now, I'm sure there are some people who read that sentence and said, "Wait a minute, I know some very effective mangers with huge teams." You may even be one of those managers yourself. But the two key words in that sentence are *effective* and *direct.* This is the whole question of span of control, and it applies to front-line managers all the way up to CEOs. Case in point, there was an interesting article from *Forbes* several years ago that reported that the average CEO had 7.44 direct reports (Myatt, 2012).

As a personal example, several years ago I ran the business consulting team for a large technology company. This team ranged between 35 and 45 people at any given time (depending on new hires and turnover) and consisted of everything from new consultants fresh out of college to senior managers with 30-plus years of experience. Each person had their own unique needs and interests. While I had administrative responsibilities for all those people, being the day-to-day go-to for any question or issue that each of those people might have was beyond overwhelming. It wasn't that I didn't like helping them—there just weren't enough hours in the day to take all their calls and all their e-mails on every little thing, and still take care of the other responsibilities that go along with being a leader in a large corporate entity. Not only was it driving me nuts, but I was also shortchanging those folks who worked for me because I didn't have the bandwidth to give every person's individual problem the attention it deserved. As anyone who has ever worked for me will tell you, that is the one thing I try very hard to never do.

To help address this issue, I set up an informal mentoring program where I took my top six managers or senior managers and assigned each of them five to seven mentees. While I still had responsibility for administrative tasks like approving vacation and time sheets, each member of the team who was a mentee would first go to their mentor for other issues. If the mentor couldn't help, only then did I get pulled in.

Making this change had several huge effects on the way the team operated. First, everyone on the team was able to develop a direct personal relationship with someone they could trust. Second, I was able to see which of my mentors embraced these added responsibilities, which allowed me to easily identify who I could recommend for promotions and other leadership roles and who I could not. The third effect was that I did not go nuts. This meant that instead of chasing around every little issue anyone had, I was able to spend my time working on how to make the team better.

What can we learn from this example? The first takeaway is that we have to recognize that to be successful and happy, we can only take on so much. The irony, of course, is that to be successful, particularly in a corporate environment, we have to expand our influence. That can mean more responsibility, more sales revenue, or bigger projects. Regardless of what outcomes we are responsible for, we have to grow our influence to keep moving forward. To do that effectively, however, we have to learn to delegate. Show people what to do, give them the resources to do, and share the credit for the positive outcomes. It will grow you, and it will grow your team. Focus on becoming a leader who manages *through* your team, not *to* your team. You'll do a better job and you'll go less crazy.

And just for the record, this by no means applies only to work. If you are a parent of a large family, don't try to do it all! Give the kids chores as soon as they are big enough. Let them learn some responsibility and help make you less crazy. I know a few parents who take great pride in telling their kids that expanding their home workforce is the main reason they had them. I don't recommend telling them that, but *do* teach them how to accomplish tasks, because it will make your life—and theirs—easier in the long run.

The second takeaway that helps us become more successful and happy is that showing you can effectively delegate will accelerate your climb up the corporate ladder. Most managers in most organizations feel like they have too much on their plate. They may not admit to it, but they do. One of the quickest ways to make yourself invaluable to your company leadership is to take things off their plate and make their job easier. This will demonstrate that you can lead and manage, and will also help make you look like you're ready for the next step in your career. Make sure you get credit for it or you may get lost in the shuffle, but you have to show that you can work with and develop others to keep progressing.

******

There are a lot of different types of people in the world. To achieve our goals, we must learn how to effectively deal with those different folks. Most importantly, we must learn to deal with people as individuals, appreciating their unique talents and abilities to contribute, not just as members of some group or another. There is a lot of talk these days about the value of diversity and the social justice imperative of embracing it. Even if you're not the kind of person who values that ethos, you should value diversity for the purely selfish reason that having a plethora of different kinds of people in our lives increases the skills, experience, and perspectives we have at our disposal. The more varied the resources (i.e., people) we have access to, the more likely we will be able to handle a lot of different scenarios.

But how do we do this? How do we learn to value different kinds of people who might bring perspectives that are divergent from our own? We do this by learning to recognize and manage our biases and stereotypes. We don't want to be limited by our prejudices and presumptions. Before we can manage and mitigate them, however. we must first understand what stereotypes are and how they develop, and recognize why it is so easy for our brains to fall back on them.

In the simplest terms, stereotypes are mental shortcuts about people and things based on a surface-level dynamic. For example, we might assume that someone who is very tall would be good at basketball. While that might be true, it also might not. Another stereotype might be assuming that someone wearing a red shirt at Target works there. That misidentification has actually happened to a friend of mine several times. He likes wearing polo shirts, and his favorite color is red. He has several of them. More than once while shopping at Target, people have assumed he works there even though he does not. He has learned to find the humor in it, but originally he found it very confusing.

Understanding why we would make such assumptions (and these are the bad kind of assumption, by the way) is a key part of understanding what stereotypes are and an important first step in managing them. Our natural default to using stereotypes evolves from two facts. First, our brains are designed to be as effective and efficient as possible. They want to be able to process information as quickly as possible, with as little input as possible, and waste as little energy as possible. As such, it is a biological compulsion for brains to try to find mental shortcuts whenever they can. Under normal circumstances, these shortcuts are non-conscious, and researchers like to give them fancy names like *default clustering* to try to explain the mechanisms (Chen & Bargh, 1997; Wheeler & Petty, 2001). But we're not worried about all that terminology here. We just want to recognize that our brains are driven to adopt stereotypes because we are, frankly, wired that way. Unless, of course, we make a conscious decision not to do that, which we will discuss shortly.

The second fact is that we all know, at least implicitly, that peoples' past behavior is the best predictor of their future behavior. For example, if our friend Joe has been late a lot in the past, we can predict that Joe will probably be late a lot in the future. If Sue has known the answer to our questions about the work processes in the past, she will probably know the answers in the future. Unless something dramatically changes, such as Joe getting in some major trouble for being late or there being a major change to the work process that Sue is not informed about, these individuals' behavior is likely to remain consistent.

The issue, however, is that while the "past behavior predicting future behavior" paradigm is relatively true for individuals, it is not always appropriate to apply this logic to people based on characteristics that make them part of some particular group. Going back to our example of tall people being good at basketball, why might we think this? We may have known a couple of tall people in the past who were good at basketball. We may watch an NBA game and notice that most of the players on the pro teams are atypically tall. Considering these two points, and our brains' penchant for mental shortcuts, when we then meet very tall people, we tend to assume that those individuals are good at basketball. This, unfortunately, is a really bad thing to do.

When we apply stereotypes (positive, negative, or otherwise) to individuals based on group characteristics, we not only make unfair and possibly inaccurate assumptions about that person, we also treat them unfairly (Goodwin, Gubin, Fiske, & Yzerbt, 2000; Wheeler & Fiske, 2005). Going back to our tall person and basketball example, the individual in question may lack athletic talent and be embarrassed when we try to get them to play. They may not even like sports. They may have other talents (e.g., music or science) that they do not get a chance to get a chance to display. Worse yet, when we allow ourselves to be caught up in stereotypes, *they* may stereotype *us* as being part of a particularly undesirable group—that group being known as *assholes*.

How do we avoid this trap? The first thing we have to do is recognize that our brains want to stereotype, and it is perfectly natural to do so. We all know people who claim they never stereotype anyone and don't hold any biases, but if we listen closely to what they say and how they act, those are often the people who stereotype others the most. Much like we talked about in our *2nd Assumption* where we are going to turn into the worst example of our parents unless we actively work not to, we must accept that we *will* default to stereotyping people… and then work to not do that. Otherwise we'll do it quite often, even though we claim we don't.

One of the clearest examples of this involved a couple of visiting professors when I was in grad school. They extolled their highly evolved virtues and declaimed about how that kept them from stereotyping other people. They then proceeded to make lots of what we would now call micro-aggressive comments toward several groups and began blatant stereotyping of people from "the south." Given that we were in Chicago suburbs at the time, I guess they assumed that there wasn't anyone from the part of the country who might be in that class. Long story short, during a break I privately and politely shared with them that I was from the part of the country they had spent the previous hour disparaging, and provided some examples of where their insights might not quite be accurate. They seemed genuinely surprised when they realized that they had been displaying the exact biases they claimed to resent. Obviously, self-awareness is the first step in this process.

This, naturally, leads to the second thing we have to do, which is learn how to listen and how ask questions so that we can get to know individuals *as individuals*. As we already discussed, each individual is unique, and while there may be some parts of them that fit within some stereotype (e.g., the tall people and basketball example), it is inappropriate and counterproductive to make that assumption. Make the effort to learn who the person is and what they are really like as an individual, and our brains' biological urge to stereotype will quickly be overridden.

****

Notice that in the discussion above about getting to know people, I put "listening" before "asking questions"? That was intentional. Learning to listen more than we talk is an important part of working well with other people. There is an old saying among personal coaches about having two ears and one mouth. The idea is that nature made us to listen twice as much as we talk. I even heard one person claim that they read "some study" about how that was nature's way of trying to make us better people or something. While I haven't been able to locate that supposed study, most of the ones I *have* found by evolutionary biologists usually posit that having two ears is more about echolocation than effective communication. Despite that, the point about listening more than we speak is a valid one. And it is valid for two very important reasons.

The first is that when people talk, they tell you about themselves—whether they mean to or not. Even when someone is trying to be all mysterious and play things close to the vest, they still reveal things we need to know to interact effectively. What they talk about reveals their interest and agendas. How they talk tells us about their emotional state. If they talk fast, they may be excited or nervous. If they talk slowly, they may be bored or tired. If they pause a lot and ask the same thing over and over again, they may be confused. Keying in on these cues allows us to get to know them better and be more effective in how we interact with them. Moreover, there has actually been neuroscience-based research showing that when people feel like they can share this kind of information, it leads to increased liking of those they are sharing with and an increase of social bonds (Ward, 2013).

This increased liking and enhanced social bonds ties directly to the second reason we need to listen more than we talk: When we do this, people will like to be around us. I know it sounds crazy, but when people feel like they can talk to you about things that interest them, they enjoy being around you more. The more they like being around you, the more effective your interactions will be. And let's be honest, there is no topic that anyone likes better than themselves. As such, when we interact with other people, we should remember to let them tell us about themselves. Unless they are some CIA-trained spy or something, they will be more than happy to oblige.

Does this mean we have to always let other people talk about any crazy thing they want, whenever they want? Sort of, but not really. Sometimes people may say crazy racist or sexist things that we don't want to be associated with. Sometimes they may say things that are inaccurate to the point of putting people in danger if those points are taken as facts. In those cases, we do of course want to step up, offer a correction, and try to get them on the right track. Use reflective and active listening to understand what they said and why they said it. Sometimes you may even find that the exact words used had a different meaning than they intended. But remember to pick your battles wisely, because every crazy thing that other people say or do seems like a good idea in their own head. This forms the basis of our *6th Assumption.*

6th Assumption: It Seemed Like a Good Idea at the Time

Like many children, one of my favorite excuses when I got into trouble was "I didn't mean to." My flawed logic was that if I didn't *intend* to create the undesired outcome, I couldn't be held responsible. My parents, however, never quite bought into that reasoning. One of my mother's favorite sayings was, "I'm sure you didn't mean to, but you didn't mean *not* to." It wasn't until I got older that I realized what she meant by that. She was asking if I bothered to reasonably consider the possible outcomes of my decisions, and if I had taken appropriate steps to avoid the negative result. Whenever she posed that question, I knew I was in *huge* trouble and there was nothing I could say or do to get out of it.

As a child, and even as a teenager, I hated that reasoning. As I've gotten older, I've learned to appreciate it much more. I've also realized that I am not the only person to whom this defense seemed like a good approach. My own children (my oldest is seven as I finish this book) have become very adept at trying to play this card, and I've honestly lost track of the number of times grown people who have worked for me have tried to use it. Every time this happens, I hear my mother in the back of my head saying, "I'm sure you didn't mean to, but you didn't mean *not* to."

The reason this question is so powerful is that it is incredibly rare for anyone to intend for something to turn out in a way that is harmful to them. In fact, if someone bothers to take any action, there is a pretty good chance that it seemed like their best possible option at some point in time. If you look up interviews with people who have won the Darwin Awards (often awarded posthumously for obvious reasons), those who knew the *winners* almost always say that they did not think things were going to turn out quite the way they did. They usually expected them to go really well. This, then, is further support for our *6th Assumption:* that no matter how foolish something seems in hindsight, *It Seemed Like a Good Idea at the Time.*

Understanding and managing this assumption is critical both for how we deal with ourselves and how we deal with other people. We have to remember that *success is never an accident, and failure is never on purpose.* As we discussed earlier, we may think someone else just got lucky, but there was probably a lot of hard work and sacrifice that came into play that we never see. Conversely, we may see someone down on their luck and think they just didn't try hard enough, or made unwise decisions. This is an effect commonly referred to as "fundamental attribution error." It occurs when we attribute our own success to our hard work and our failure to external influences—but make the exact opposite attribution when evaluating other people (Langford, Beehr, & Von Glahn, 2017). When we do this, we forget that success and failure are rarely the result of any single decision, but rather the accumulation of the results of several decisions. Without exception, there were early decisions that seemed like good ideas.

One of the more explicit illustrations of this principle comes from the paradox of drug and alcohol addiction. Ask any elementary school student what they know about drugs and alcohol and most will say they are bad for you. Why? Because significant effort has been put into sharing this info in our schools. Yet every year, new people become addicted. While I have been fortunate enough to avoid struggling with addition myself, I do have several close friends and family members who succumbed to it. One friend in particular, who is now an extremely accomplished professional and business owner, went through a major bout of drug addiction in his younger days.

He's now a father whose oldest children are getting close to the age where they are likely to be exposed to those temptations.

One day when we were talking, the subject of drugs and alcohol came up and I asked him what he planned to say to his kids when they asked about his experiences and his history. I honestly expected him to say that he was going to simply lie to his kids as so many parents do. I was completely caught off guard when he said, "I'm going tell them the truth. I'm going tell them they were fun." After being stunned for a second, I asked him if that was really such a good idea, although I may have said it a little less politely than that. He laughed for a minute, then explained his plan to me:

> I'm going to tell them they were fun the first time you do them. I'm then going to tell them that they became very unfun very, very fast. I'm going to tell them about the hell I went through while I was using. I'm also going to tell them about all the pain I went through while I was trying to quit. How much I lost in the process, and how much work it was getting clean and sober. I'm going to tell them about all the times I relapsed before it finally stuck. I'm also going to tell them how hard it is staying clean and sober now, all these years later. If that doesn't

scare them enough to stay away from that crap, then there isn't a whole lot I can do.

Now, for the record, I am not an addiction counselor or a child development specialist. My expertise in those areas is limited to what we learned in the joint classes with the clinical psychology students in grad school, and having been on a few dissertation committees that cover related topics. As such, I am really not qualified to comment on whether this is the right approach, or if it matches up to what the standard addiction avoidance protocols say. What I *will* say is that this is coming from someone I have known for many years and whose opinion I've grown to trust and respect. It is also someone who does a lot of work helping other addicts through the recovery process. He freely admits that he never set out to become an addict; he was just having fun. Before he knew it, though, things got out of hand. This is not unlike the teenager who didn't mean to get pregnant, or the suburbanite who didn't mean to have a wreck and get a DUI after a few glasses of wine after work. These folks didn't mean for these bad things to happen; they simply didn't mean for them not to.

How do we avoid this? Let me start by saying that it is tricky. So tricky, in fact, that I'll be the first to admit that there have been a number of times when I myself have not been so successful at it. There have been a number of decisions in my life that I realized were suboptimal after the fact. Some I realized many days or weeks later; others I realized a split second after I started executing, but there was no way to course-correct. Everyone has done this, and most of us are likely to do it again at some point in the future. The goal is not to eliminate such mistakes, as that is impossible, but to reduce them to a manageable level and to make sure the ones you have are just annoyances that are a pain in the neck to deal with, not major negative impacts on your success and happiness.

The first step is learning to think of life like a chess game. Does this mean we have to learn to play chess and understand all the different strategies that go on in a particular match? Not unless you want to. Chess is a fun game and if you find some good folks to play with, it does train your mind to think ahead. But you don't have to be all into it to use this approach. What you do have to do, however, is learn to think about more than just your next move. This is true in a chess match just like it is in everyday life.

While there are rumors that chess grandmasters can think 10-plus moves ahead, Grandmaster Maurice Ashley points out that this is not possible, as there are something like 318 billion possible combinations in just the first four moves of any chess match (2012). No one's brain is capable of foreseeing all that. What grandmasters do, however, is learn to recognize different situations and try to make sure they take the steps up front to move the game toward the outcome they want. Unlike many people who think only one or two moves ahead and then react to what the other player does, the grandmaster has a clear endgame in mind and manages the environment on the board toward that end. This is directly related to our discussion of systems thinking we touched on in our *5th Assumption*. The way we avoid problems is to think about the endgames we want and actively work to manage our environments toward those goals.

Let's say you're a student with a big test the next day, but there is also a show you really want to watch on television. If you're thinking like a lot of people, you'll say "I want to watch this show. It starts at 8 p.m., it is over by 10, and then I can study before I go to bed." What many people forget to consider is that we aren't going to go straight from the show to studying. Most of us will waste at least half an hour messing around after the show before starting to study again. Also, if we start late, we will likely be tired and not really able to absorb any of the new material because all we'll be thinking about is wanting to get to bed. Given this chain of events, we probably won't do so well on the test.

If we're thinking like a chess grandmaster, we'll work backwards on this and say that if we want to do well on the test, we'll need to study for at least two hours. We also recognize that the last time we tried to "study after doing something," we were not able to concentrate because we were tired and thinking more about sleep than study. We'll then realize that the likelihood of being able to accomplish both goals if we watch the show first is pretty low. That will then lead us to look for a way to make them both work… a simple win-win is to set the DVR or see if the show will be available on demand. We'll study now, and watch the show later. That would be a much better decision, all because we could recognize the pattern of what we were going to do and make a better decision based on logical reasoning.

How do we learn to recognize these patterns? The answer reminds me of an internet meme I saw recently that said to be "old and wise," one must first be "young and stupid." While I usually prefer to phrase things a bit more positively, I have to admit that the point is valid. To become wise, we usually have to learn from our mistakes. We are all going to make mistakes. Some are big, some are small, but we all make them. In fact, I have a rule that I never trust any successful person who claims that they've never made a mistake or failed at anything. They either completely lack self-awareness, or they are lying. For those who have self-awareness, we understand that the most important part of making mistakes is learning from them. The trick, of course, is to not dwell and not to let them hold us down but to use those mistakes to lift us up to new knowledge. How do we do this? We use what I like to call the LLM strategy:

- **Look at it:** Figure out what happened and why the suboptimal result occurred.

- **Learn from it:** Understand what could have been done differently and why that would have made a difference.

- **Move on:** Once you have finished looking at it and learning from it, don't worry about it again except for implementing the lessons that help you avoid it in the future.

What too many people do, however, is to dwell without learning. They kick themselves for being "stupid" and ruminate on the less-than-ideal decisions they've made. This creates what systems theories call "reinforcing loops," which are bad enough for groups, and even worse for people (Senge, 2006). This approach is suboptimal because all is does is make whatever bad thing they did seem worse, causing them to lose confidence in themselves when making future decisions. For obvious reasons, this doesn't do anyone any good.

Instead of doing this, accept that you made a mistake, figure out what you could do differently if you find yourself in a similar situation in the future, and then just move on. The only exception, of course, is if your actions impacted someone else. If they did, apologize, try to fix what you can, and get on with trying to do better next time.

****

That last point is a really important one, because in the same way our suboptimal decisions may impact others, other people's suboptimal decisions may impact us at some point in time. Returning to our *5th Assumption*, no person is an island, so no matter how hard we try, we're going to have to deal with other people and the decisions they make. While it is easy to deal with other people when we think they are making good decisions, we are also going to have to deal with them when they make bad ones, too. And for better or worse, all the stuff they do seems like a good idea at the time. One of the key parts of our *6th Assumption* is learning how to deal with others when they do certain things when we think they should have known better.

Over my years as a management consultant, I had several colleagues who were just plain grumpy. Usually these were senior technology guys (and I say "guys" because a much higher percentage of the senior tech people that I dealt with were male) who just didn't have a lot of patience for other people. While I know there are certain personality profiles that are more common in some jobs than others, I'm honestly not sure if that job attracted these kinds of folks or if the job made them that way. What I do know is that it seemed to be a common theme. One of the odd things about working with these kinds of individuals is that their grumbles often masked interesting pearls of wisdom. The trick is filtering those insights through all the less useful criticisms. One of my favorite was from someone we'll call Charlie (not his actual name) who used to like saying, "Never underestimate the stupidity of your fellow human beings."

Granted, this was not the nicest thing to say, but it did make an important point: Just as we are all bound to make some mistakes at some point, other people will too. Some will be small. Some will be big. Some won't affect us. Others will create huge messes that we have to clean up. Regardless of the kind of mistake, the question we have to consider is: How do we deal with other people's mistakes? Remembering that the only two things we can truly control are our actions and our attitudes, there are two answers to that question.

First, we have to try to learn from other's mistakes just like we do from our own. For example, when reading biographies about famous business leaders like Steve Jobs or Jeff Bezos, we need to make sure we don't just look at the high notes. Most people merely look for the inspiration of going from the basement to the billionaire suite and ask how they can do that, too. What they forget, however, is that just like we talked about in our previous assumptions, becoming successful is not a linear process and no one who is successful got there without falling down a few times. As we mentioned earlier, Steve Jobs was such a pain in the neck to be around that he got fired from the company he founded, and it wasn't until he learned to work better with others and came back that Apple really soared (Isaacson, 2011). And he is by no means the only example.

We have to ask what happened when these successful people fell down. Why did they think that the approaches that got them in trouble were the right idea at the time? What did they learn from those experiences? In the same way that chess grandmasters learn to recognize patterns from their own games, they also learn to recognize patterns by studying other people's games. Learn to study the games of other successful people and see what patterns they learned from so you can learn from their mistakes before you make your own.

The second thing we have to do regarding other people's mistakes is to learn be gracious and pay our success forward. For those who believe in karma, this is one of the most important parts of becoming successful and happy. There are times when we're not doing too well, and we hope that others will help us. By the same token, we should be ready to help others when we are doing well and they are not. This is because when we are successful, we have an obligation to make sure we take the time to help others learn from their own mistakes, as well as from the mistakes and successes of other people.

As we've already discussed, it is a pretty safe bet that almost no one sets out to mess up. Sure, there are those rare times when someone might *take a dive* to achieve some longer-term goal, but even then it is part of a larger plan that they think will work out in the end. When that goes wrong, they are usually not sure what to do next. Moreover, they are probably pretty embarrassed and left feeling foolish. As such, our place is not to judge or criticize but to help them learn. How do we do this?

First and foremost, we have to remember that just like everything you do seemed like a good idea to you, everything that others do seemed like a good idea to them at some point in time. For example, I have another good friend who is a recovering addict; he has managed to stay clean and sober for more than a decade and half. Prior to that, he went through several very scary years. He's a smart guy, and he knew on some level that doing drugs could lead to bad things—he obviously wasn't someone who didn't know any better. Like a lot of people, he drank when he was younger, and even smoked some cannabis on occasion, but it wasn't until he was a young adult that he tried "the hard stuff" and things went really bad.

When I asked him once what led him to even try his drug of choice in the first place, he shared with me the very messed-up place his head was when he started down that road. He had lots of issues going on in his life at the time; some of which I already knew, and some were shocking surprises. At the moment of that first bump, the temporary release from the anxiety and the stress was a welcome change. It also didn't help that the party culture in the town where he lived was like something out of a bad '80s movie. As such, there were plenty of drugs floating around in his circle and at first, people were more than willing to share. It was initially very enjoyable and didn't seem like a burden. Pretty quickly, however, there were other anxieties and stresses in his life, meaning more drugs for the same release, and the addiction took over. He almost lost everything. He never thought he would become addicted; he just wanted to a release from his stress and to feel good for a moment. That is frankly what sucks a lot of people in.

This is only one example of how big mistakes usually start off as little ones. Another example could be someone who cheated on a spouse. The marriage was having issues, then someone else paid them attention they weren't getting at home. A friendly ear over drinks leads to a few more drinks and lowered inhibitions and they make a big mistake. It could be someone who took a few extra write-offs on their taxes. One year it is a couple hundred dollars. The next year it is a couple thousand. Then there's an audit. It could be someone who simply drove too fast and got a speeding ticket. Regardless of what the exact mistake is, we've all done things that were not good ideas, and we all have friends and colleagues who have done unwise things. Given our *5th Assumption* that no person is an island, and our *6th Assumption* that it all seemed like a good idea at the time, the question is, how do we deal with those folks so that we can pay it forward?

Above all else, we don't talk down to them. We don't berate them. We don't tell them they are dumb, and we don't tell them they were foolish. Odds are they already think that. What we actually need to do is offer what psychologist Carl Rodger called *unconditional positive regard*. This means the warm and genuine acceptance of the person's experiences, particularly when they are trying to make a consistent positive change in their life (Bozarth, 2013). In other words, we accept the person even if we don't like what they have done, particularly when they are trying to be better. For those who are Christians, this is very similar to the biblical directive to hate the sin but love the sinner. Does this mean we have to accept those who are genuinely bad people? Not at all, and those are not who we are dealing with here. What we are talking about here are good people who make mistakes.

Once we provide this *unconditional positive regard*, we then work with the person to help identify where they went down the wrong path. We try to help them see why their logic at that key time was flawed. We try to help them figure out if there is anything that can be done to correct the situation. We also help them figure out what they can do to learn from the situation. We may even learn something ourselves in the process. The goal here is to make sure they don't make the same kind of mistake again.

We do this because it is the right thing to do. And even you're the selfish kind who doesn't care about other people, you should do it because one day you're likely to mess up, and you hope someone will do the same for you. That, of course, is assuming we make it a point to surround ourselves with the right kind of people, which is a key point in our 7th and final assumption.

7th Assumption: You Will Become Who You Surround Yourself With

There is an old saying that you will become the five people you spend most of your time with. This is a favorite maxim of multi-level marketing organizations (e.g., Amway, LegalShield), as they are trying to convince you to spend more time with the people in that organization than with others. Another version of this that I heard the one time I tried my hand at direct marketing was "scientists have proven that you can calculate a pretty good estimate of someone's annual income by averaging the annual income of their five best friends." I find this version to be particularly amusing because I am one of the scientists who study these kinds of issues. To be honest, I have searched all over the place for a study that says something even close to that, but have yet to find it. This does not necessarily mean that it doesn't exist, but I have not been able to locate it in any of the scientific literature, despite significant effort.

While there may be a lack of an empirical support for a formula to calculate someone's net worth based on their local peer group, it is true that who we surround ourselves with has a huge impact on what we do and how we act. As such, who we surround ourselves with significantly contributes to how successful and happy we become. This is why parents are always telling their children to stay away from that "bad crowd." It is also why one of the first rules of being released from prison on parole is that you cannot hang out with your old associates from before you were incarcerated. When you talk to folks who are in addiction programs like Alcoholics Anonymous, they say one of the most important parts of recovery is learning to spend more time with people who don't drink than with those who do. This is because we adopt the habits, behaviors, and opinions of the people we spend most of our time with. So if you want to learn how to have fun without drinking, you need to hang out with people who know how to have fun without drinking. By the same token, if we want to be happy and successful, we need to associate with others who are also happy and successful.

Why is who we associate with such an important part of our success? To explain this, I'll share that in high school I was what you might call an "Olympic hopeless" in cycling. By this, I mean that at the time, I thought I had a shot, but in truth I had none. I'm not sure that I had the legs or the lungs, and I definitely didn't have the focus or the discipline. What I did have were some good friends that I rode with who were much more talented. A couple of them ended up winning national titles, and I have heard that one of them briefly raced professionally. I thought that if my buddies could do it, I surely could too.

While I didn't win nearly as many races as I had hoped and certainly didn't achieve my overly ambitious athletic goals, I did learn some important lessons from those experiences. Some of those lessons were about the normal things that kids get from sports, like the importance of hard work, goal setting, and all that stuff. Other lessons were things about tracking progress and understanding that improvement is not linear, and it doesn't just happen overnight. One of the most important lessons, however, was that if you want to get better at something, you need to be around people who are better at it than you are.

In the case of a sport like cycling or running, that means that if you want to get faster, train with people faster than you. You'll hate life while doing it. You'll be in the back of the pack a lot, which I often was, but you will be better once it is done. You will also begin picking up the habits and norms of that group, and that will help as well. You'll eat like they eat. You'll train like they train. And you'll learn about the strategies that are required to be a champion. As we discussed in our *3rd Assumption*, life is always in progress, and success is often a matter of changing your habits. Being around people who are what you want to be is a major enabler of changing those habits.

Another great example of this important concept comes from the 17 years I spent working in the management consulting industry. For those who don't know, there is a pretty significant amount of diversity in terms of the capabilities and training of those who call themselves consultants. There is everything from single-shingle "consultants" who found themselves in that role after being laid off from a regular job and fell into some contracts that they somehow managed to keep going. There are also large 394,000-person technology firms that do multi-million-dollar contracts for industry and government. The most prestigious consulting firms are the 3,000 or so person strategy firms that hire hotshots right out of top-tier colleges and MBA programs, groom them to be the best of the best, and then fire some percentage of the lowest performers every year to make room for new blood. It sounds harsh (and it can be), but it creates an environment where only very smart and very talented people last more than a few years.

During my career, I actually managed to spend time as single-shingle contractor, employed by a couple of the super-large technology firms, and even do a couple of years at one of the super-prestigious (yet harsh) strategy firms. While at the strategy firm in my mid-20s, I began discussing what it took to become a partner with a partner I was working under. I knew that if I was going to stay in that industry, I wanted to make partner. I figured one of the best ways to find out how to become one was to ask one, so I decided to pick his brain about what it took to make it.

One of the more interesting pieces of advice he shared with me was to never be the smartest person in the room. At first, I thought he was talking about just an impression management thing, where you don't want to show off too much because people might see you as a threat or a challenge to their position. That was not it. In fact, in that environment, you had to show off how smart you were on a daily basis just to survive, but that is a separate issue. What he was talking about was making sure you were always around people who were smarter, more experienced, and more talented than you. The first reason for this is so that you can learn from them. Not just in terms of specific tasks, but so you can learn their habits, learn their patterns, learn what they read and how they act. You want to try to emulate them so that you can emulate their success.

The next reason you want to surround yourself with people who are smarter than you is because at some point, you are going to have a problem that you don't know how to solve. Most smart people like helping other people. Some do it to be good people. Some do it to show off. Some do it so you'll owe them a favor. Regardless of the person's motivation, when you find yourself with that problem, just ask for help. But don't merely ask them what to do. Ask them why they think their solution is the best solution and how they came up with it. The goal here is to learn how they made those high-quality decisions. If you stay in a place where you are the smartest person in the room, there is no one to ask for that kind of growth-enabling help.

The last reason you never want to be the smartest person in the room is because no organization runs on just one person. Sure, there are some people who have a bigger impact than others, but at the end of the day, it is always a team effort. While it is not critical that everyone in the room be smarter than you, if there is only one smart person, that group is probably not going to last very long. The single smart person will quickly get burned out from carrying the load and seek a better group. The original group will then fall apart. Perhaps this was the logic behind Groucho Marx saying he said he would never join any club that would have him as a member.

Obviously, there are some pretty big benefits to making sure we surround ourselves with the right people. The question we have to ask, however, is how we can use this to also make ourselves happy. As we established with our *1ˢᵗ Assumption*, success is a self-defined social construction. Once we get past being happy, paying our bills, and not being a burden on others; what counts as success for one person might be different from what meets that definition for another. One person may want to be a musician, another may want to be a stay-at-home parent, and another may want to be some kind of scientist. Happiness is different for each of us and we'll have to learn individually how to get where we want to be. One way to gain the knowledge we need to achieve these individualized goals is to use what my lovely wife likes to call her *circle theory.*

To understand *circle theory,* we have to set the context that she grew up in southern California, and spent most of her time there through her mid-20s. As a result, she was well acquainted with quite a few people in the entertainment industry. Despite the recent press about abhorrent behavior of some of the people in that industry, it has historically been very popular, and many people still dream of breaking into it. With so many people vying for so few opportunities, simply having talent isn't always enough to succeed. Many times, the decision maker has to know you personally for you to even get the chance to break in. In other words, you have to be in their circle. While this is one of the most extreme examples, every industry is like this to some degree or another. If you want to get into something and succeed at it, you have to get into the right circles.

Some people see getting into the necessary circle merely as a matter of knowing people who can do things for you. That assumption is where a lot of people go wrong. They think that if they just know people who have the ability to help, then they'll achieve their goals. They'll take all kinds of crazy steps to buddy up to the "right" people in hopes of gaining something. The problem is, the people who really have the knowledge and the power to help you can usually spot that kind of desperation a mile away and are not interested in helping those who are only out for themselves. As such, think about how *you* can help *them*, and by doing that, they'll be able to help you. There is an old saying that "givers gain" and it is especially true in this case.

The way we gain by getting into the circles that are made up of the kind of people you want to be goes back to our earlier discussion about being able to learn about them and learn from them. You want to see how they do things, how they approach things, and how they made decisions. This is the old "give a man a fish, he'll eat for a day; teach a man to fish and he eats for a lifetime" maxim. You don't want these folks to give you a fish—you want them to teach you to fish. This is similar to the apprenticeship models of job training that were common before standardized education, and which still exist today in many highly skilled trades (e.g., plumbers, electricians). The goal is to gain a circle of people who are what you want to because we become the people we surround ourselves with.

The converse of this is that you have to make sure to remove yourself from people who are bad influences. Most of us have had the experience of our parents not wanting us to hang out with someone they thought was a bad influence. When I was a teen, I thought my parents were just being critical or snobby, but now that I'm in my mid-40s, I've realized that my parents were right every single time. I can think of several instances where I didn't listen to them and later regretted it. I can also point to quite a few times when I did listen to them and was later very grateful, because those people I thought were so cool ended up somewhere I really did not want to be. We have to surround ourselves with people who support our success, not those who drag us down.

Doing this may require you to disassociate from some people you once considered close friends and that can be hard. I know it was for me the times when I've done it. But if those people aren't helping you do things that you need to be doing, it's time to walk away. Of course, if they decide to change to a more positive way of life, you can always be ready to welcome them back.

One of the more interesting examples of how our connections promote desired outcomes involves those network marketing organizations I mentioned before. Also known as direct sales organizations, or pejoratively called pyramid schemes, this is where networks of independent contractors sell some goods or services and also seek to recruit new associates into the organization. Whenever someone you recruited sells something, you get cut of that payout. This is called your downline. Whenever you sell something, the people up the chain who you were recruited through get a cut. This is known as your upline. One of the fastest growing organizations in this category right now is Rodan + Fields, which recently topped more than $1 billion in sales and has done a great job at changing the lives of people who are willing to embrace the organization and its philosophies (Dunkey, 2017).

Because these businesses are built on people and relationships, a high priority is placed on associates building personal relationships and surrounding themselves with people who have similar goals. There is a constant focus on new recruitment and creating circles of likeminded people. For the right kind of people, this is a great way to earn income and build wealth. Ironically, however, these efforts are often approached inappropriately and have left a bad taste in many people's mouths.

Long before I was born, my parents considered doing Amway. It sounded like a great way to earn extra income with good long-term potential. That part they liked. What they did not like, however, was the constant pressure to recruit. It was so bad that their upline told them that if they didn't have the kind of friends who wanted to take advantage of that business opportunity, then they needed to find a different group of friends. My father interpreted that as suggesting he should abandon his old friends, and he's just not that kind of guy. Since he thought that was his only option, they walked away. What he didn't realize is that he didn't necessarily have to do that.

While there are some people in those organizations who harass their friends and family until they give it a shot, that is a very short-sighted approach. Your options are limited to those people you already know, and you may end up alienating people who mean a lot to you. What they should do instead is take advantage of the previously mentioned *circle theory* and expand their circle to include new people who are willing to embrace the network marketing ideals and approaches. This is what the truly successful people in that industry do. And to be honest, it is what every successful person I know does in every industry. They are always looking to expand their circle and to find likeminded people they can work with and learn from.

You don't necessarily have to change all the people you surround yourself with to be happy and successful, but you may have to expand your circle. The good news is that the number of people you have in your life is not limited unless you want it to be. Expanding these circles also means that, just as we discussed in our *2nd Assumption*, you'll get to play more and more different and interesting roles.

To use myself as an example for this last point, I have some good friends who I have known since I was a kid. They're great people. I can always count on them and I wouldn't trade them for the world. They've seen me at my best and my worst and I can completely relax around them. For the most part, however, they are not that interested in discussing the research I'm doing, the classes I'm teaching, or the books I'm writing. For those conversations, I have a whole different set of friends.

Throughout my consulting and academic careers, I have accumulated an entirely different group of friends, many of whom are leading experts in their fields, are published in leading journals, and spend their days pushing the boundaries of intellectual thought. These are the folks I can go *full nerd* with. But there is also a lot of stuff that I discuss with the first group that that I would never discuss with the second. Some people may find the dichotomy odd, but for me it is an important part of living out the *1st Assumption*, regarding success being a self-defined social construction. I want to be surrounded by good friends I am comfortable with and whom I can completely trust. I also want to be able to have intellectual stimulation that I can use to create new knowledge and help others. And I also want to do it in a way where I can make a comfortable living to support my family. I achieve this by living out the *2nd Assumption* in which my life is a first-person narrative where I play different roles at different times.

With one group of people, I am Dr. Brown who lectures on transformational leadership and mentors doctoral students through their dissertations. With another group, I'm just Jimmy with strong opinions about whether our favorite college football team needs to fire its coach. What role I play more and what story I write changes constantly. That is okay, though, because it leads to a richer and fuller experience. There may have been earlier times in my life where I tried to be just one or the other, and I honestly wasn't happy or successful. Since I've learned to embrace all my various roles and surround myself with different groups of people to support those roles, I've had way better luck expanding my circles and achieving my goals. And that, of course, is what this whole journey has been about: finding ways to reach the goals that will make us successful and happy.

To do that, we must have the right behaviors. To have the right behaviors, we must have the right beliefs. To have the right beliefs, we must make good assumptions.

Closing Thoughts

Whenever I come to the end of books like this, I always find myself asking, "Okay, so what?" What are the key takeaways that I should have after perusing the previous pages? Suspecting that others might be asking the same question, I've thought long and hard about that, and the overarching theme of this text is this:

No matter who you are, no matter where you started, no matter where you are today, everyone deserves to be successful and happy.

This work has been an attempt to provide some useful and actionable guidance to work toward that objective.

Bear in mind that the belief that everyone deserves to be successful and happy does not mean that the world owes you anything. And it certainly does not owe you what you think you want to be successful and happy. It doesn't work like that. What it does mean is that you have every right, and some might say the responsibility, to make the decision to start the process to achieve your goals. To do that, you must take positive and proactive action to make it a reality.

Before taking action, you must first decide what success and happiness mean to you. Until you make those decisions, you won't be able to decide what actions will lead to the result you want. To make those decisions, you must put yourself into a mental state where you are open to the different options might be required. The best way to open yourself up to those possibilities is to accept the *7 Assumptions* in this book.

1st Assumption: Success is a self-defined social construction. Only you can truly decide what you need to be successful and happy. You also have to accept that what makes you successful and happy today might not make you successful and happy tomorrow. It is an ever-evolving process, and embracing that evolving goal makes for a richer and fuller experience.

2nd Assumption: Your story is a first-person narrative. At the end of the day, you have to decide how your story goes. You can't control other people or your environment; you can only control how you react. Make sure you tell your story in the most positive way possible.

3rd Assumption: Life is always in progress. Just like marathon runners know they have to work toward the long-term goal of being able to run 26.2 miles in one shot, our life is a marathon. Work toward the longer-term benefit. It may not pay off right away, but it *will* pay off.

4th Assumption: You are going to have ups and downs. Accept that some days will be great, and others not so great. The difference between very successful people and less successful people is that the very successful people keep going and stay positive even during the downs.

5th Assumption: No person is an island. We can't survive without other people, and we honestly wouldn't want to. We also have to manage our environment to make sure it is supporting our goals. Take the necessary steps to ensure that you are in a place where you can achieve healthy relationships and positive progress.

6ᵗʰ Assumption: It seemed like a good idea at the time. Everything that everyone does seemed like a good idea at some point in time. We have to accept that in ourselves and others. When it turns out our logic was flawed, just use it as a learning experience. When we see others making mistakes, we should try to help them learn as well.

7ᵗʰ Assumption: You will become who you surround yourself with. In the same way that we can't avoid being around other people, we have to try to surround ourselves with the people who support and uplift us, not the ones who bring us down. We also want to expand and diversify our circles to make for a more fulfilling life experience.

If we take these points in total, we can see that the first two assumptions are about how we decide what results we want. The next two assumptions are about how we take certain steps to get to where we want to be. Our last three assumptions are about how we maintain the positive momentum that comes with those changes. Maintaining that momentum is one of the hardest parts of achieving lasting success. But as hard as it is to stay on track, it is even harder to get back on track when we fall off.

One my favorite examples of someone who worked very hard to get back on track is my own father. For most of his life he had been a relatively healthy man. He spent more than 20 years in the military, ran on an almost daily basis for many years, and I remember him playing church softball and various other sports when I was a kid. He was like this at least through his early 50s. Sometime after that, however, there were several life circumstances that resulted in his gaining a significant amount of weight. So much weight, in fact, that it was negatively impacting his health and life.

On a conscious level, he knew he had to make a change, but it took a while to find success. After several false starts, he found the right motivation and the right program to drop the weight. One of the key differences of the final program compared to others was that the successful program told all the participants on day one that it was not about a diet. It was about changing your lifestyle habits to enable you to drop the weight, and do it in a healthy way. That change in lifestyle is what finally worked, and he's been able to stay in great shape for several years now. Enabling you to change your lifestyle to drive success and happiness is what these *7 Assumptions* are all about.

Does this mean I guarantee you'll be happy and successful if you accept these *7 Assumptions*? No, because there are no guarantees in life. What I will say, however, is that these *7 Assumptions* are based on lots of data collected over many years, triangulated with peer-reviewed research by leading experts and interviews with people who are modeling the outcomes we want to achieve. As such, this isn't just some guy saying that he was a great salesman and here's what he did, which may or may not work for you. It's a combination of a lot of different successful and happy people sharing their stories, even if they didn't all realize it at the time. The amalgamation of those stories creates a framework of approaches that have worked for a lot of different people in a lot of different situations. It is also a set of tools, techniques, and guiding principles to help you start down your path of becoming successful and happy. That is what you truly deserve, and what you will achieve if you decide to make it happen.

Works Cited

Achor, S. (2010). *The happiness advantage: The seven principles of positive psychology.* New York: Crown Publishing Group.

Agee, W. C. (1979). *Patrick Henry Bruce, American modernist: A catalogue raisonne.* New York: The Museum of Modern Art.

Ashley, M. (2012). *Working backward to solve problems: Maurice Ashley.* Retrieved from TED Ed: http://ed.ted.com/lessons/working-backward-to-solve-problems-maurice-ashley

Bozarth, J. (2013). Unconditional positive regard. In M. Cooper, M. O'Hara, P. F. Schmidt, & A. C. Bohart, *The handbook of person-centered psychotherapy and counselling, 2nd ed.* (pp. 180-192). New York:: Palgrave Macmillan.

Bronfenbrenner, U. (1979). *The ecology of human development: Experiments by nature and design.* Cambridge, MA: Harvard University Press.

Chalmers, A. (2013). *What is this thing called science?, 4th ed.* Indianapolis, IN: Hackett Publishing Company, Inc.

Chen, M., & Bargh, J. A. (1997). Nonconscious behavioral confirmation processes: The self-fulfilling consequences of automatic stereotype activation. *Journal of Experimental Social Psychology, 33*(5), 541-560.

Covey, S. R. (2004). *The 7 habits of highly effective people.* New York: Free Press.

Creswell, J. W. (2013). *Research design, 4th ed.* Thousand Oak, CA: Sage Publications Inc.

Darley, J. M., Glucksberg, S., & Kinchla, R. A. (1986). *Psychology, 3rd ed.* Englewood Cliffs, NJ: Prentice-Hall.

Dunkey, N. (2017, April 17). *Rodan + Fields reaches $1 billion milestone.* Retrieved from Business For Home:

https://www.businessforhome.org/2017/04/rodan-fields-reaches-1-billion-milestone/

Esar, E. (1968). *20,000 quips & quotes.* New York: Barnes & Noble Books.

Gergen, K. J. (2001). Psychological sciences in a postmodern context. *Amercian Psychologist*, 56(10), 803-813.

Goffman, E. (1959). *The presentation of self in everyday life.* New York: Anchor Books, Doubleday.

Goodwin, S. A., Gubin, A., Fiske, S. T., & Yzerbt, V. Y. (2000). Power can bias impression processes: Stereotyping subordinates by default and by design. *Group Processes and Intergroup Relations*, 3(3), 227-256.

Hatch, M. J., & Cuntliff, A. L. (2013). *Organization theory: Modern, symbolic, and postmodern perspectives 3rd eds.* Oxford: Oxford University Press.

Isaacson, W. (2011). *Steve Jobs.* New York: Simon & Schuster Paperbacks.

Kuhn, T. S. (2012). *The structure of scientific revolutions: 50th anniversary, 4th ed.* Chicago: The University of Chicago Press.

Langford, S. J., Beehr, T., & Von Glahn, N. (2017). Mistakes abound with ingratiation in job applicants: Attribution errors and gender bias. *The Psychologist-Manager Journal*, 20(2), 59.

Miller, G. A. (1956). The magical number seven, plus or minus two: Some limits on our capacity for processing information. *Psychological Review*, 63 (2): 81–97. doi:10.1037/h0043158.

Myatt, M. (2012, November 5). *Span of control: 5 things every leader should know.* Retrieved from www.forbes.com: https://www.forbes.com/sites/mikemyatt/2012/11/05/span-of-control-5-things-every-leader-should-know/#5ee78db728c8

Olsen, J. (2011). *The slight edge.* Dallas, TX: SUCCESS Books.

Robbins, A. (2003). *Awaken the giant within: How to take immediate control of your mental, emotional, physical and financial destiny!* New York: Free Press.

Schultz, D. P., & Schultz, S. E. (2016). *A history of modern psychology, 11th ed.* . Belmont, CA: Wadsworth.

Senge, P. M. (2006). *The fifth discipline.* New York: Doubleday.

Statistic Brain Research Institute. (2016, October 1). *Marathon running statistics.* Retrieved from StatisticBrain.com: https://www.statisticbrain.com/marathon-running-statistics/

Ward, A. F. (2013, July 16). *The neuroscience of everybody's favorite topic.* Retrieved from www.scientificamerican.com: https://www.scientificamerican.com/article/the-neuroscience-of-everybody-favorite-topic-themselves/

Webster's. (1996). *Webster's II New Riverside Dictionary Revised Edition.* Boston: Houghton Mifflin Company.

Wheeler, M. E., & Fiske, S. T. (2005). Controlling racial prejudice: Social-cognitive goals affect amygdala and stereotype activation. *Psychological Science*, 16(1), 56-63.

Wheeler, S. C., & Petty, R. E. (2001). The effects of stereotype activation on behavior: A review of possible mechanisms. *Psychological bulletin*, 127(6), 797.

Wohn, D. Y., Peng, W., & Zytko, D. (2017). Face to face matters: Communication modality, perceived social support, and psychological wellbeing. *Proceedings of the 2017 CHI Conference Extended Abstracts on Human Factors in Computing Systems* (pp. 3019-3026). Denver, CA: Association for Computing Machinery.

Wood, J. V., Heimpel, S. A., Newby-Clark, I. R., & Ross, M. (2005). Snatching defeat from the jaws of victory: Self-esteem differences in the experiece and anticipation of success. *Journal of Personality and Social Psychology*, 89(5), 764-780.

About the Author

Jimmy Brown, PhD, is an author, educator, and management consultant with more than 20 years of experience helping organizations and individuals achieve peak performance. During his career, Dr. Brown has worked around the globe and held senior-level consulting positions at several marquee firms. He is a frequent speaker on the topics of business strategy, organizational change, and peak personal performance. Dr. Brown is an adjunct professor with several universities' psychology and management programs and is regularly sought out for his insights on how to practically apply cutting-edge theory to solving real-world problems.

Dr. Brown's previous titles include *Systems Thinking Strategy: The New Way to Understand Your Business and Drive Performance* and *Journey Management: Unleashing the Strategic Power of Change.*

www.jimmybrownphd.com